BE YOURSELF SALES

How To Sell Your Services Without Selling Your Soul

Peter Brodie

Copyright © 2020 Peter Brodie

All rights reserved

The characters and events portrayed in this book are fictitious. Any similarity to real persons, living or dead, is coincidental and not intended by the author.

No part of this book may be reproduced, or stored in a retrieval system, or transmitted in any form or by any means, electronic, mechanical, photocopying, recording, or otherwise, without express written permission of the publisher.

ISBN-13: 9798633387254
ISBN-10: 1477123456

Limit of Liability/Disclaimer of Warranty. While the author has used his best efforts in preparing this book, he makes no representations or warranties concerning the accuracy or completeness of the contents of this book and expressly disclaim any implied warranties of merchantability or fitness for a particular purpose. No warranty may be created or extended by sales representatives or written sales materials.

The advice and strategies contained herein may not be suitable for your situation. You should consult with a professional where appropriate. The author shall not be liable for any loss of profit or any other commercial damages, including but not limited to special, incidental, consequential, or other damages.

To Lisa…for putting up with me
To Mum and Dad……for putting up with me
To Max, Ruby, and Isla………for putting up with me

WHAT OTHERS ARE SAYING

"Peter's approach to getting more clients is practical and simple. The results speak for themselves; this is the best month in my coaching consultancy. My client base is now expanding across the globe. Thank you"

JAZMINE WOLF, FOUNDER AND DIRECTOR OF A LIFE COACHING ORGANISATION

"I can't recommend Peter highly enough. His support and guidance over the last couple of months have been invaluable. Buy this book!"

CHRIS WELLARD, MANAGING DIRECTOR OF A MANAGEMENT CONSULTING COMPANY

"Be Yourself Sales is a practical, easy to follow and refreshing in its approach to getting more clients. I highly recommend it."

STUART MITCHELL, PROGRAMME AND CHANGE DIRECTOR, FREELANCE

"Consultants and Consultancies should checkout Peter Brodie's approach to helping you get more clients. This book will deliver great results."

RICHARD DALEY, DIRECTOR OF STRATEGY AND TRANSFORMATION OF A LARGE GLOBAL CONSULTING FIRM

"Be Yourself Sales Coaching with Peter is the best investment I have ever made. I would thoroughly recommend Peter's BYS approach to any consultants and coaches wanting to win more business."

OWEN BENNET, INDEPENDENT OPERATIONS AND SUPPLY CHAIN SPECIALIST

"I had the pleasure of being one of Peters first pupils in developing my knowledge and understanding of Be Yourself Sales. Peter is an excellent coach and mentor that guided me through my understanding of this way of thinking and how it links targeted strategic growth with tactical intervention."

JOHN POWELL, DIRECTOR OF OPERATIONAL EXCELLENCE OF A CONSULTING FIRM

"I highly recommend this book, and at least a conversation with Peter...engaging, no-nonsense and Be Yourself Sales really works."

TERRY MURPHY, FREELANCE STRATEGY CONSULTANT FOR ENVIRONMENTAL CHARITIES

CONTENTS

Title Page	1
Copyright	2
Dedication	3
What others are saying	5
Be Yourself Sales	11
Introduction	13
Building Brands	16
Constructing Credibility	36
Positioning Pricing	61
Managing Marketing	77
Commencing Conversations	103
Preparing Proposals	120
Winning Work	144
Planning Progress	188
Personal Power	203
Appreciating Adventures	224
The Framework	242
Index	247
About The Author	250

BE YOURSELF SALES

"Be Yourself; everyone else is taken"

OSCAR WILDE

INTRODUCTION

It was the early 2000's, and I was feeling pretty proud of myself. After 25 years of hard work, I'd been promoted to Managing Partner of a large global management consulting firm. This was it—my ultimate career goal.

Unsurprisingly, my new role brought with it a shift of priority and responsibilities. My focus was now on retaining current clients, expanding live assignments and attracting new opportunities. In short, I had to grow the business.

I started by reviewing the company's sales reports. It wasn't pleasant reading. The firm's sales were flatlining—we weren't shrinking, but we weren't growing either. Worryingly, over 80% of our revenue came from two clients and our other revenue streams were stale. There was no vitality in the sales pipeline and if we were to lose one or, God forbid, both of the main clients the business would be in serious trouble.

Reviewing the situation highlighted two other big problems: I was not a natural salesman, and the firm's consultants didn't know how to sell our services. Moreover, their attitude was that to sell consultancy you had to be smooth, confident and, dare I say, posh. And they were none of these things.

I could only see one way forward. I would have to go out and learn from the best salespeople in the world, use this knowledge to design our own approach and then teach and coach the staff on how to get more clients. If the firm was to grow, the team had to grow professionally—we couldn't be reliant on a few prima donnas, high-maintenance sales directors. Everyone had to get involved.

I decided that it was better for 100 people to take one step than for one person to take 100 steps.

My subsequent study of sales methods revealed that historically there are three main approaches to selling professional services: salesperson focused (it's all about me), client focused (it's all about you), and system focused (it's all about the process). It soon became clear that, by themselves, none of these methods is enough. They felt outdated, prescriptive and unsuitable for coaches and consultants.

I knew that clients no longer wanted rehearsed elevator pitches or cheesy sales scripts that looked and sounded like everyone else's. They didn't want to be bombarded with sales messages on LinkedIn. They wanted relaxed, genuine and authentic conversations with an expert about their challenges and ambitions.

I sat down and drew a ten-by-ten matrix, and in it I compiled everything I had learned: what clients wanted, what the salesperson should do and say and the mechanisms required to form a productive approach. By the end of the exercise, after several iterations, I had a 10^2 framework for selling coaching and consulting.

The new approach was an instant success. The consultants felt comfortable promoting and selling our services, we attracted new clients and the firm grew. More than anything, the difference was that the team felt they could sell successfully without being pushy, slick or cocky. They could just be themselves.

I now teach coaches and consultants to sell effectively using the Be Yourself Sales framework. As its name suggests, it's not a mechanical system that should be followed blindly. It's a structure that can be populated with your own individual skills, experience and personality. There's no 'one size fits all solution'—that's the whole point.

The number one attitude that will change the way you sell your services and grow your business is to be yourself. Don't try to be somebody you're not or wouldn't like to be. This changed the way my sales team worked back then and has changed the way my clients sell today.

You have the ability to promote and sell your services just as well as anybody. You can attract and retain as many clients as you need or want. You might feel uncomfortable, hopeless or perhaps even depressed by your inability to grow your business. No matter what you think is stopping you, the lessons in this book can be applied to your situation. And whether you're an independent coach working directly with clients, an associate working through another company, or a consultant working within a consulting firm, the framework has the flexibility to make it your own.

The 10^2 approach consists of ten steps that teach you how to build your brand, construct credibility, position your pricing, manage your marketing, commence sales conversations, prepare compelling proposals, and of course, win the work. To make the approach sustainable, the framework also sets out how to plan and manage your progress, draw on your own personal power to stay focused and motivated and, last but not least, how to appreciate the adventure. Because there's no point doing all this unless you are enjoying yourself. After all, happy people sell.

If you're sick of prescriptive selling techniques, this book is for you. If you don't like the idea of trying to be a slick salesperson, this book is for you. If you don't know how to promote and sell your services, this book is for you. If you don't have an approach for training your team to grow the business, this book is for you. If you don't understand why all your hard work is not generating the money you deserve, this book is for you.

Getting more clients than you could ever imagine doesn't have to be difficult, stressful or high-pressured. It can be natural, fun and authentic. You just have to take a few steps and learn how to tap into the unique and natural talent that is yours alone—being yourself.

Let's get started.

BUILDING BRANDS

What

Articulate clearly and simply the sector you specialise in, what your services are and the benefits they will bring your client.

Why

Consultants and coaches tend to describe what they do in one of two ways: using vague and mystical terms or in excruciatingly dull detail. In both cases, the client will be none the wiser when you reply to the "what do you do?" question.

How

If you want your potential client to remember you, be clear, concise and relevant. Pinpoint the types of people you want as clients and research them to understand their challenges and ambitions. Then align your services to address their needs and desires.

❋ ❋ ❋

It's 4 am. It's cold, dark and raining outside. You're dreading going out to face the elements for the jog you promised yourself last night, but you know you must. As you put on your training shoes, there is a sudden, strong urge to go back upstairs to the warmth of your bed. But you push the feeling to one side and step out into the cold, clean air. Thirty minutes later, you return home invigorated and thankful you were able to take that first step.

In many areas of life, the first step is the hardest. However confident you are, you'll have experienced that feeling of trepidation before you start something new. But why is it so difficult to get going?

In my experience the main reason people hesitate or avoid taking the first step is the fear of failure. And the root cause of that fear is that the end goal itself seems too big and difficult to achieve.

If an overweight person (I could use myself as an example) was told by their doctor to lose 100 pounds, that patient might be overawed by the scale of the challenge. 100 pounds? Where would you even start? But if that doctor broke it down to losing one pound per week, the patient would find it more achievable.

The same applies to your challenge of getting a steady stream of clients. It might seem like an unachievable goal. That's why the Be Yourself Sales framework is a 10^2 matrix—each of the ten chapters is broken down into ten manageable steps. Together they form a straightforward guide to getting more clients, one that can be achieved without feeling overwhelmed.

Step 1—Identify Your Market

A target market defines the group of people you provide your service for. The typical categories that are used to break it down are sector, industry, business size, location and job function. A target market is used to identify the potential clients to whom you want to promote and sell your services.

Identifying your target market is an essential step in developing a marketing plan. Not knowing your target market will prove costly and consume a lot of your time because, as the term suggests, it's the group of people you're going to target your marketing towards.

How many clients do you need each year? Five? Ten? Thirty? Whatever your answer is, I doubt that it's hundreds or thousands. Yet I see so many consultancies doing 'wide-blast' marketing to tens or even hundreds of thousands of people. Why market to so many people when they need so few clients? It's not necessary, and in most cases it looks and feels like a vanity project.

No doubt you've heard this before. We both know that identifying your market is the first step to getting enough of the right business. I know it, you know it, everyone knows it, and we advise our clients to do it, too. Yet most consultants and coaches aren't carrying out this fundamental step. They're not taking their own medicine.

You might say, "But I like working in a variety of sectors, it keeps my work interesting. My approach and skills can be applied to a wide variety of industries." Of course, that might be true, but if you go down this path you'll be considered a generalist. There are lots of generalists out there, most of them competing on price, and if you adopt the generalist approach you'll be competing for the same work as many others with nothing to differentiate you from your competition.

In these situations, the balance of power will always be in your client's favour because there are so many choices available to them. When the client holds the upper hand, prices will always be pushed downwards. And as we know, it's near impossible to build a profitable and sustainable professional services business based on cost alone.

If, on the other hand, you define your target market, you'll show those people that you're dedicated to and knowledgeable about their situation. Do you want them to think of you as someone who'll work with anyone with a cheque book and pen or someone who's dedicated their professional career to working with people just like them?

If a potential client thinks you understand their precise situation, nine times out of ten they'll choose the specialist.

One more thing. If you still think defining your market will restrict your opportunities, remember this: groups of people talk to each other. They establish formal and informal networks and connections. They recommend and refer. This web of people could leverage and multiply your promotional activities, as they talk to others in their industry with the same problems and desires.

To pick a target market, the first step is to identify a range of potential groups that need and consume your services. Then select the most relevant market to focus on. Try to identify ten to fifteen potential target markets, then use these questions to whittle them down to the most attractive:

What sectors and groups of people use the services you provide?

Which of these do you have the most knowledge about?

Which of these have you provided services to before and have a track record in?

In which of these have you produced the best results for your clients?

Which of these contain people who could be future clients?

Which of these do you enjoy working with the most?

Answering these questions will give you a good idea of a suitable target market.

Step 2—Define Your Client

Even when you've defined your target market, it doesn't mean that all those people are suitable clients for you to work with.

In my early days of working as a freelance management consultant I worked for some terrible clients. However negative they were, I was always professional and polite and did a good job, but it wasn't my best work. I didn't try too hard to extend the assignment and was always looking for a quick and clean exit. I was desperate to find better, more satisfying and enjoyable clients but was too busy with my less-than-perfect existing ones.

Why do we do it? Why do we agree to work with clients we know won't be good for us and our reputation? It all boils down to the same reason we become generalists and spread our services far and wide: lack of confidence.

There will always be an oversupply of generalist consultants and coaches relative to client demand. To counter this, you should present yourself as a confident, trusted, credible expert in a specific field. Having a niche will put you in a place where demand exceeds supply and you can command higher fees.

Aim to work with a sub-set of people within your chosen target market. Who is your model client? We've all had good and bad clients, but have you ever sat down and reflected on the specific traits that made one person a joy to work with and others so very painful?

Lift your sight and go beyond settling for *poor*, *average* or even *good* clients. Accept that only the *best* client is good enough for you—the ultimate model client. It takes a hefty dose of courage to say "no" to those who don't meet your criteria, but it will serve you well in the long run.

What happens when you work with model clients on your assignments? You do your best work, produce the best results for them, and of course, enjoy the work most. So, avoid clients who are not ideal and focus on attracting the people who suit you. If you fill your schedule with not-so-good clients you'll have no space to take your dream customers on when they show up.

Companies, sectors and environments change often. An individual's personality, beliefs and characteristics change less frequently.

By focusing on your model clients, your marketing will gain a level of longevity.

To help discover your ideal client's characteristics, write a list of all your previous and current clients. If you're just starting out and haven't had a client before, write a list of all your former bosses. Remember: clients are individual people, not their companies. Now ask yourself these questions:

Who did you get the most job satisfaction from working with and why?

Who did you have the most fun working with and why?

What is their approach to work?

How would you describe their personality?

You should now have a good idea of what's worked well for you. Now ask yourself the same questions, but this time look to the future.

Who do you want to work with going forward?

What are the characteristics of a model client that would provide you with a high level of job satisfaction?

What type of person would you enjoy working with?

What is your ideal client's approach to work?

How would you describe your perfect client's personality?

Asking these questions about previous and future clients should help define your model client. These are the people you're going to work with in the future. If you're still stuck, ask yourself this straightforward question: what client characteristics will stop you doing your best work and will you not accept from this point onwards?

Step 3—Understand Their Situation

Once you've settled on your target market and defined your model client, you'll be able to research their requirements. Study this small group of people, pinpointing the situations they're facing and the direction they want to go. Remember that there are only two main reasons a client will hire a consultant or coach: fear or desire.

Fear means that either something bad has happened or is about to happen and the client is worried. They're facing real or future challenges, and these will be in the front of their mind. They want to tackle them as a priority, and your job is to move them from a negative place back to a neutral point.

Desire means they want something they don't yet have. They have ambitions—things they want to achieve in the future. These might not be pressing, but they should be worked towards in the medium term. Your job is to move them from a neutral place to a positive point.

Some clients have either fears or desires; the majority have both. This means that for most clients your job is to move them from a negative position all the way to a positive. So, assure your clients that not only will you solve their current challenges, you'll help move them towards their ambitions.

If your sales approach involves identifying and understanding your clients' negative challenges and positive ambitions, everything changes. Your discussions with potential clients improve, and how you describe what you do changes for the better. You're regarded as an experienced expert who knows and has dealt with people just like them facing problems just like theirs. If you understand their challenges and ambitions, you'll gain credibility.

If you don't know these things, how are you going to promote your services? How can you talk to potential clients with authority about what they need and want?

Do some research on your target market and the ideal clients within it. You should be able to answer these questions:

What are the top five challenges your clients face—the things they are worried about?

How are these challenges affecting their current situation and performance?

If they are to address their challenges, what does a return to 'normal' look and feel like?

What are the top five ambitions your clients have—the things they desire?

How will these ambitions effect their future situation and performance?

If they were to achieve their ambitions, what does 'success' look and feel like?

Once you've identified their challenges and ambitions, validate them by finding other research and reports that correlate with your thoughts. It's not enough to jot down what you *think* they are based on your experience.

If you do your research, when you write or talk about your client's situation, everything you say will resonate with them. They'll think, "This person gets me, they understand me."

Step 4—Define Your Services

It's Valentine's Day. A young couple in love goes out for a meal. They walk into a restaurant hand in hand and a waiter shows them to their table, where they sit, gazing into each other's eyes. Time passes. After a little while, they realise that the waiter hasn't brought them a menu, so they call him over.

"Excuse me, please, can we have a menu?"

The waiter looks down his nose. "Sorry, Sir, we don't have menus. You tell us what you want and I'll go into the kitchen to see if we can help you."

What would you do in this situation? How would you feel? I'm pretty sure you'd feel confused and left in the dark. And yet this is the approach many coaches and consultants adopt.

Your services are not your profession. "I do lean", "I'm a life coach" and "I'm a management consultant" are all good and well but whatever your profession, job title or technique, these aren't the services you offer.

When consultants promote their expertise but not their services, it's a bit like that waiter who offered an unlimited menu. It's like saying, "Tell me what you want and I'll tell you if I can do it." That approach doesn't work in the restaurant trade and it doesn't work in the professional services sector either.

Describe your services in terms that address the client's challenges and ambitions. Your services don't need to be unique and tailor-made for each client—in fact, it's uncomplicated to design a standard service that works for all of them. If you've done your research and understood their fears and desires, you'll know what they need and how you can help.

Let's say you're a management consultant working in the healthcare sector. You're an expert in improving the performance of A&E departments. Both you and your clients already know what the problems and future strategies are. So, it's easy to design a set of services that help. They might be:

A diagnostic service that tells the client the root causes of lengthy patient waiting times.

A design service that improves the flow of patients.

An implementation service that helps the client put the solution in place.

You as the specialist consultant already know what is involved in providing each of these services. You also know the average size of an A&E department. If you know these things, it should be easy to articulate the service, what's involved and how long it takes. Here's what that might look like:

"I offer a diagnostic service that identifies the root causes of a patient waiting times in A&E. The approach uses a method called value stream mapping and it takes ten days to complete."

Compare this to:

"I provide unique solutions designed to suit the problems you might have. I work with lots of different organisations, so I need to spend some time (and your money) to orientate myself. My approach is to meet you and talk through your situation. I'll then go away for four weeks to meditate in a darkened room to pull a strategy out of thin air that's never been tried in a department like yours. I'll then use my magic fairy dust to conjure up the answer I think you'll like, even if it's not the right thing to do. The whole process will take somewhere between four weeks and four years."

As far-fetched as this sounds, I'll bet you recognise at least some of the elements in the message this puts across.

Who would you choose to work with? The pragmatic expert who specialises in your field and provides a clear, straightforward service? Or the wizard who can fix any problem in any department but you'll have to wait four weeks to find out how?

Defining your services means being able to say, "I understand your challenges and ambitions, I've seen them before, and this is how I can help you address each of them".

Do some research. Understand your client's challenges and ambitions, the fears and desires they have, the challenges they face and what they want for the future. Then align your services to them, describing what each service does, how it is performed and the average time it takes to do it.

Step 5—Pinpoint The Benefit

Now that you know what your target market is, the problems they need to address in the short term and what they hope to achieve in the longer term, you can pinpoint the primary benefit you provide for your target market.

I say 'primary' because this is the single most significant benefit you produce for your clients. It's your niche, what you are known for, and the reason clients hire you.

Lots of people say things like:

"I help people…" To do what?
"I improve performance…" Which aspect?
"The team implements lean…" For what purpose?
"We improve employee engagement…" Why?
"I make you stronger…" To go on to do what?

These promises are too general; they don't spell out what the client gets when they hire you.

Most assignments have one significant outcome the client is looking to attain. It might be to reduce costs or bring a transformation programme back to plan, or to raise someone's confidence. Ensure the benefit your services bring is precise, simple, succinct and easy to understand without any interpretation.

The primary benefit my clients get from working with me is getting more model clients. What's yours? Here are some examples you might find useful:

"I help people lose weight."
"I improve on-time delivery performance."
"We reduce factory costs."
"We reduce staff turnover."
"I help employees return to work."

These examples are specific—the client knows what they are paying for and what to expect.

Now it's your turn. Define the most significant benefit clients get from working with you. Make it simple and straight to the point with no ambiguity. Also remember to keep it short—ideally it should be no more than eight words.

Step 6—Articulate The Outcomes

The benefit your services give to your clients is the punchline that grabs their attention. But that benefit also brings broader and deeper advantages. These are the additional outcomes, and to articulate them you need to think through all the other positive stuff the client gets from hiring you.

Let's retake my example. The primary benefit I provide is to help consultants and coaches get more clients. The additional outcomes that come from that include being able to charge higher fees and bring in more money. Your sales cycle will also be quicker, your levels of stress lower, and you will be in a better place physically—to name but a few.

If you're a personal fitness coach, your primary benefit might be to help clients lose weight. But I'm sure there is a wide range of deeper and broader outcomes that flow from that. More confidence, nicer clothes, feeling happier within yourself... the list goes on.

When you think of the additional outcomes of your services, think as long-term as you can. If your primary benefit is to reduce factory costs, the client will have lots of options on how to use that extra cash. They might increase profits, invest in new equipment, lower prices to get more work or share the windfall with the employees.

Grab some paper and a pen and list the additional outcomes your clients will enjoy from working with you.

Step 7—Categorise The Outcomes

If you've completed the above exercise thoughtfully, your

list of additional outcomes may stretch to thirty items or more. It's a lot to remember. To help your clients understand and remember all these outcomes, it helps to categorise them into logical sub-groups. I call these the five Es:

Economy: What are the direct financial benefits and return on investment your clients can expect?

Effectiveness: What tasks, processes, or people will become more productive or dependable?

Efficiency: What elements will flow quicker and smoother?

Emotional: How will people's feelings, passions, sensations and mental health change for the better?

Environment: How will the physical environment, working areas and individuals' physical health improve?

List all the benefits and then categorise them in one of the five Es above, then pick the top two or three from each category. You'll be able to explain to clients the full range of outcomes they'll get from your services. When they see it like that, it will make an impact, and they'll be more likely to remember what you say. Here's an example:

"The primary benefit you'll get when you work with me is retaining your biggest customer, who's threatening to leave. As a result, we'll safeguard your revenue and reduce your costs. Your customer order fulfilment process will be more reliable and have a quicker turnaround. We'll do this by reorganising the shop floor to be more productive and a nicer working environment. I wouldn't be surprised if the staff become more loyal when they hear that the contract with the customer has been extended for another five years."

This is a pretty attractive and convincing offer, isn't it? And all because the consultant has identified the single most significant benefit they produce and then categorised all the other positive outcomes. If you don't do the same, you risk being bland, confusing and unclear when you describe why clients should work with you.

Step 8—Explain Your Purpose

Clients buy your services for a range of reasons. It could be because of the combination of benefits you provide or because you're an expert in your field. Or perhaps it's because they like the methodologies you use. Or it be might be a combination of all three.

But sometimes a client buys your services because they've connected with you on a personal level. To turn this around the other way, they won't use you if they don't like you. They want to feel their work and personal views align with yours, and this is why both you and the client will find it valuable if you can articulate your 'why'.

What it is that drives you to get up every morning and serve these people? Why have you chosen to do what you do?

Clients make buying decisions based on logical and emotional reasons. They want to know the outcomes and benefits, but they also want to know why you are in your line of work and why you work with people like them. If these two things resonate with your prospective new client, then you're 80% of the way to winning new business. Try answering these two questions:

Why have you dedicated your professional life to working with your target market and model clients?

Why are you in this line of work, what is that motivates you, what led you down this path?

Note down your answers and be ready to open up to clients during informal conversations. Remember: you're a human being and not a consulting machine, and it will serve you well if your client knows it.

Step 9—Build Your Brand

All the work we've done so far is a stepping stone to building your brand. Use your responses from the previous steps to form the backbone of your brand and be the springboard for your promotional activity. It helps to write it down, so get some more paper and start jotting down how you would complete these seven statements:

Statement 1—Who you serve (your target market)

My example: I coach service professionals, usually consultants and coaches.

Your answer: I help/coach/advise_____

Statement 2—Where your clients are located

My example: The majority of my clients are management consultants found in the UK, although I have a few located in Europe and Asia.

Your answer: My clients work in_____ sector and are found in _____

Statement 3—Your client's typical challenges and ambitions

My example: There are four reasons my clients work with me: 1. They don't know how to sell or feel uncomfortable selling their services. 2. They are successful freelancers but rely on associate work through other consultancies so get paid only half of what the client pays. 3. They are only able to command low day rates and want to know how to raise their fees. 4. They have no clients or not enough clients and want more.

Your answer: My clients reach out to me for these reasons_____

Statement 4—The services you provide

My example: I offer two services: 1. Individual one-to-one coaching for private clients. 2. Group coaching for corporate clients. In both cases I teach and coach people how to authentically get more clients using a structure designed specifically for consultants and coaches. I call this the Be Yourself Sales framework.

Your answer: I help my clients address their urgent needs and achieve their future ambitions by_____

Statement 5—The primary benefit you achieve for your clients

My example: The number one benefit I provide is that I help people get more clients.

Your answer: The number one benefit I provide is_____

Statement 6—The additional outcomes your clients enjoy

My example: There is a range of follow-on benefits that come from getting more model clients. Economy: income will increase as your schedule fills up with work and you can command higher fees. Effectiveness: you will be able to focus on your primary services that provide value for your clients rather than losing too much time to sales activities. Efficiency: the time it takes to win new clients will decrease as prospective clients will flow through your sales process quicker, more reliably and more smoothly. Emotional: imagine how it would feel having that burden removed, knowing there is plenty of high-value interesting work queuing at your door. Environment: This will generate more free time that you could use for leisure or reinvest back into your business.

Your answer: There are a range of more extensive benefits that stem from (the significant benefit). These include (use the five Es): _____

Statement 7—Your 'why' (your purpose)

My example: You know, the whole reason why I started this business was to help people just like you. After decades in the consulting sector, I grew concerned just how hard service professionals struggled to establish themselves, feeling the disappointment of not succeeding, when they could have achieved their dreams with a little help.

Your answer: The reason I am in this line of work is_____

Most people do not do enough work on the third statement (challenges and ambitions), and yet it is one of the most important. If you want people to perceive you as an expert in your field who knows their sector inside out, you'll need to spend time researching your target market and model clients. Then you'll be able to define and understand their current challenges and the pressing problems they're experiencing.

Do the same research to identify and understand your clients' future ambitions—the things they desire and want to achieve in the future or the things they want to move towards.

Go through these statements and fill in the blanks and don't forget to try several versions until you are happy. You can even test them by saying them out loud. Which one sounds best?

What do you feel most comfortable saying? What feels most authentic?

Bring these statements together to build your brand—the who, where, what, when, why, and how of your business. When you put yourself in a position to communicate your brand naturally and authentically you'll find yourself using it everywhere: not only on your website, LinkedIn profile and promotional materials, but in your discussions and proposals as well.

Step 10—Practice Having Discussions

Gone are the days when you had to create a script or sales pitch to sell your services. Customers have long cottoned on to the fact that people who do this are following a pre-planned monologue, and they simply switch off and stop listening.

Consider each of the statements in step 9 as a 'module' you can use on its own or combined in various formations to suit a situation. How you use them will be determined by how much time is available for the discussion with your prospective client and the environment you're in when you meet them.

Here are a few combinations to think about having up your sleeve:

A short version. This condensed option might be apt when meeting someone for the first time, perhaps at a conference when time is limited. Combine the first and fifth statements: who you work with and the significant benefit you help them achieve.

A medium version. A longer version than the one above might be more appropriate when you have a little more time in a more relaxed atmosphere, perhaps at a dinner party or a working lunch. Combine the first, second, fifth and sixth statements: who you work with and in what sector/location, the significant benefit you help clients achieve and the additional outcomes (the five Es) that come from attaining it.

A more extended version. Use this when you have the time and space to have a meaningful conversation, perhaps at a formal business meeting or in an informal discussion when you are sitting next to someone on a train or taking a flight. You can use all seven statements in this setting. Take your time, and don't try to fit all seven in one long monologue. You could start with the first and second statements to say who you work with, then develop the conversation by talking through the third and fourth statements to expand on the challenges and aspirations of your clients and the services you provide.

Later you can talk through the fifth and sixth points, to explain the primary benefits you help your clients attain and the additional outcomes that flow from this. You can then connect with them on an emotional level by opening up about why you do what you do.

You can use many combinations of these statements depending on the circumstances. It's up to you, just be yourself. However, it's essential not to use them as a standard script. These statements are 'modules' that you've crafted to be succinct, interesting and informative; they're to be woven into a friendly, authentic conversation.

Most coaches and consultants haven't done this preparatory work and talk only about the approach or methodology they use. But clients don't buy technical models and methods. Clients buy people and results. At the deepest level, clients want to know, "Can this person help me?"

Tell your clients who you work with so they know it's people just like them. Help them realise that you understand their challenges and ambitions so they know you can help them. Put a spotlight on the significant benefit they'll gain from your services so they know there'll be a healthy return on their investment. Put the icing on the cake by describing the broader range of additional outcomes. And connect with them emotionally by sharing your why.

Finally, practise these statements until they flow naturally.

Nothing beats saying them out loud to yourself in front of a mirror, as you'll pick up what sounds good and what doesn't. Ironically, the more you practise, the less rehearsed it will sound, and you'll come across as relaxed, confident, knowledgeable and experienced—the characteristics a client looks for.

❋ ❋ ❋

Ten Steps To Build Your Brand

    Step 1—Identify your market
    Step 2—Define your client
    Step 3—Understand their situation
    Step 4—Define your services
    Step 5—Pinpoint the benefit
    Step 6—Articulate the outcomes
    Step 7—Categorise the outcomes
    Step 8—Explain your purpose
    Step 9—Build your brand
    Step 10—Practise having discussions

CONSTRUCTING CREDIBILITY

What

Establish yourself as a credible expert in your field and continue to build your reputation with clients.

Why

The first question a client will ask before hiring you is, "Can this person help me deal with my challenges and achieve my ambitions?" You need to construct credibility if their answer is to be "yes."

How

Before you start promoting your services, get the basic credibility builders in place. Then put into practice the things that will delight potential clients and build credibility and trust.

❋ ❋ ❋

Understanding what clients value when looking to hire a consultant or coach will help you establish what aspects of your service and sales cycle construct or destruct your credibility.

But how do we know what's really important to our customers?

In the 1980s Professor Noriaki Kano studied the factors that influence customer requirements and designed a framework called the Kano model. For this chapter I've taken the standard Kano model and modified it to suit your needs of selling consulting and coaching.

The Kano model is based on the idea that there are several categories of feature in a product or service. Some will build your credibility and others won't. Understanding them will help you focus on what's important.

Assumed credibility builders

These are the things you don't talk about or specify to your clients. That's because they're so basic that clients expect them. They won't give you any additional credibility as they're taken for granted—a basic set of features that you're expected to have. But if you don't have them in place, their absence will reduce your credibility, usually to the point that potential clients will write you off.

Imagine booking and staying in a hotel room. When you arrive you can see that the room is clean. The hotel's website didn't tell you it would be clean, but you expected it as a minimum standard. If it wasn't clean you would certainly not be happy at all, but as it is, you barely notice. That's because as a feature it's assumed.

Agreed credibility builders

These are the features that you and the client have talked about and agreed to. Many of these elements will already have been defined when building your brand—they include things like who you work with, the primary benefits of your service and the broader range of outcomes.

Additional credibility builders could be formed during your

initial conversations when you tell your client what you do and they tell you what they need. They might be performance elements, such as reducing waste by a certain percentage. These are specified benefits and outcomes you'll help the client achieve. The proposal you prepare for the client state these, and you both sign the document to formalise the agreement.

Take the hotel room. Say you booked a twin room to be available from 2 pm. As you specified these two requirements when booking the room, if they're not met you won't be happy. If they are, you'll be satisfied.

Delighted credibility builders

These are the items that the client does not articulate or define as they are not expected. It doesn't matter if you don't have delighters in place or you forget them, as the client wasn't expecting them in the first place. Your credibility will be intact. But if you provide them, they'll be delighted, as you've gone above and beyond what was anticipated. Delighted clients supercharge your credibility.

It's the equivalent of finding two small chocolates on the pillows of your hotel bed, or discovering that the beds have been turned down when you return in the evening. You didn't specify or expect this, but you're delighted it's been done. As these things were beyond your expectations, you'll have a positive memory of the experience, and tell your friends about this charming hotel. But if they hadn't provided that extra service, you wouldn't be dissatisfied as you didn't expect it in the first place.

Unconcerned credibility builders

These are the elements clients don't care about. If they're present or absent, it makes no difference—your credibility is unaffected. So if you're spending time and money on something that means nothing to your clients, question why.

For example, your hotel room might have an expensive, complicated alarm clock with five different sounds. You don't care what sound it makes as long as it wakes you up, and in fact you don't care if there is an alarm clock at all, as you can use your mobile phone. This example highlights the ever-changing expectations of clients: a few years ago, an alarm clock would have been an assumed expectation, but today is considered an unwanted extra.

Reversed credibility builders

These are the factors that cause you to lose credibility when present but construct it when absent. This phenomenon is rare, but it does happen.

For example, your hotel room might have a window with a view. But the view is of a back alley, where you can see the staff door to the kitchen. The chefs are outside smoking, and you can see rats running around the pavement. You have a room with a view, but the view diminishes the hotel's credibility.

The 'assumed', and 'agreed' elements are must-haves for your business. If you don't have them, their absence will destruct your credibility. The 'delighted' features are nice-to-haves—if you don't have them, their absence won't create doubt, but if you do, you'll construct your credibility and be known as a trusted expert in your field.

Step 1—Get Yourself Sorted

You need to have the assumed credibility builders in place before you start your marketing efforts. If you don't, people won't consider you a professional and an expert in your field. It's important you put all of these things in place before you start—if you take short cuts and any are missed, nothing else will matter.

If people are to take you seriously, the first thing you need to do is get yourself a decent photograph and email address. You might scoff, but you'd be surprised how many dodgy photos and email addresses you'll find when you scroll through LinkedIn.

Clients don't ask for these as they are already expected. You know you should have them in place. If you haven't got round to it or have done it but in a haphazard or unprofessional way, get these items sorted as a priority. Technology makes it easy, quick and cheap to get them in place to a standard that isn't too far from what large companies pay millions for.

You might say, "I know, of course I need to have these things in place—it's obvious. I just haven't had time to get them done." Maybe you've been busy, or you've been relying on work as an associate. If you're a freelance service professional or a company associate, the company you work for will certainly have these things in place. But the price you pay for being reliant on others to get clients is around 50% of your fees. Think about it. Let's say your clients are charged £1,000 per day for your services. You'll receive £500, and the firm you work for retains the other £500. They profit from you. Now let's say you've worked this way for five years. If we also assume that during this time you've been busy but not working every day, it might work out that you've worked an average of 200 fee-earning days per year. That equates to 1,000 fee-earning days over the last five years.

I'm sure you can do the math. 1,000 days losing £500 means that you have lost £500,000 over the course of the last five years. Half a million pounds. If you had worked with your own clients over the last five years you could have earned one million pounds—you would have been a millionaire. All because you took some time to get these standards in place and constructed your own personal credibility.

Let's start with photographs. You'll use these for a range of purposes: your LinkedIn profile, your website and your biography to name a few. Don't be tempted to rummage around your personal photographs to find the one you like best and think nobody will notice. You know the pictures I'm referring to: the one when you were on holiday and had a great tan, or the one at your sister's wedding when you wore your favourite dress.

And don't be tempted to use photographs taken by the companies you used to work for. Again, people will know what you've done. I used to work for a consultancy that had a standard dress code including an orange tie. When I first started my coaching business, I recycled the old photograph of me. The orange tie was a giveaway, and people recognised it and knew it was an old photograph.

If you use a photograph that was taken five or ten years ago, when you meet your prospective client they might not recognise you. Grey hair, a few extra pounds and, dare I say it, more wrinkles on your face that are not on your photograph will not serve you well. Coming across as inauthentic or dishonest is not a good impression.

Use a professional photographer. They'll know how best to portray you and will produce a range of quality pictures for you to choose from. I would suggest you stick with close photographs, capturing your head and shoulders or head and torso. If you're too far away, people will struggle to see you clearly on social media, especially if viewed on a mobile phone.

Avoid cheesy, staged poses. Sitting in a fashionable chair looking serious, standing in a power pose with your hands on your hips, using a cartoon avatar or pointing at the camera will not do. You'll look fake, disingenuous and downright silly.

Using a professional photographer is inexpensive and will set you apart from other coaches and consultants. Your photograph is the first thing potential clients will see, so make it as good as possible.

Next, get a professional email address. Why, oh why, do professionals still use personal email addresses? Let me tell you straight: it makes you look like an amateur. Even worse is to have a witty email address such as snakehips@blueyender.com or easypeasy@gmall.com. Your email address should consist of your name and your company name, and that's it. Mine is peter@byscoachinggroup.com - nothing fancy, nothing funny and nothing unprofessional.

Step 2—Establish your presence

Another assumed credibility builder is a simple, professional and modern website. The web domain name should match or be close to your email address and should follow the general rules above: nothing funny, unprofessional or unexpected.

You don't need a large, corporate-looking website with lots of pages. All it needs to do is tell others who you are, what you do, the benefits you give your clients, some testimonials and your contact details. If you've done the work in chapter one, Building Brands, you'll have already created a lot of this content.

Your next assumed credibility builder is having a presence on LinkedIn. There are many books on how to create a top-notch LinkedIn profile; don't waste your time and money on them. All they do is state the obvious, and you know what a good profile looks like—it's just that you haven't invested the time to do it.

Your LinkedIn profile should include a professional photograph, a statement about the group of people you provide services to and what you help your clients achieve. It should be a simple statement, to the point and easy to understand. Leave no doubt about who you work with and what you do.

Make sure you also have a company page on LinkedIn. It reinforces your credibility and your logo will show up in your work experience section. Your company page also serves as your shop window, where prospective clients will look before deciding to contact you. This page should be concise and mirror much of the content of your website. Be mindful about what you post as well, as when prospective clients look at your profile; they will dig around. If you've made embarrassing or controversial comments, you'll lose their interest in seconds.

Step 3—Create Standard Materials

As well as having a digital presence, there are some materials you must have in place before you start to promote your services. These include a company brochure, service overview documents, client testimonials and a biography. All of these are assumed credibility builders that clients will expect you to have.

The information within a company brochure should describe who you are, why you do what you do, who you provide services to, the challenges they face, the benefits your service offers, how you work with clients and a statement on why they should work with you. Think of your brochure as a condensed, paper version of your website and LinkedIn profile.

When a potential client becomes aware of your services and is in a position where they might need them, they will come and check you out. They'll ask themselves one simple question: "Can this person help me deal with my challenges and help me achieve my ambitions?" A powerful way to demonstrate that you can is by having testimonials showing how you've helped lots of others before.

Most testimonials don't contain enough information to demonstrate the service provider's ability to deliver the goods. I see too many make vague statements like "Bob did a great job; he helped us improve. I would not hesitate to use his services again". The quote is attributed to a set of initials or simply a position within the company.

This kind of testimonial isn't going to have much credibility, and it's not going to get people queueing up to hire you. A real person with a real name from a specific company provides a good testimonial, but most clients won't have time to write a good one. To get the information you need to create an excellent testimony without them having to work too hard, ask your clients these questions:

Can I use your name and company for a testimonial?

What were the circumstances that made you look for support?

Why did you choose me?

What were the benefits and outcomes I helped you achieve?

Are there any positive comments about my approach you would like to make?

Would you use my services again?

If so, why?

Here's an example of a simple yet powerful testimonial:

> *"We received notification from our customer that they had found defects in the products we make for them. Bob worked with our team to improve the quality of our fuel pump manufacture. He raised our right-first-time measure from 91% to 99% in one month. We could not have done it without him.*
>
> *The improved quality also reduced productions costs, and our customer has given us more work as a result.*
>
> *Bob adopted a hands-on approach from day one and coached with all our team members to improve our processes."*
>
> JOHN SMITH, MANAGING DIRECTOR OF XYZ PUMPS LTD.

The higher the profile of your testimonials the better. If Bob received a testimonial from Toyota or Apple, wouldn't you want to work with him? Testimonials can feel bland and mundane and may not serve as a real differentiator if they're not from recognised individuals or companies. When the time is right, ask all your clients for specific, positive feedback about you and your work. Then write up their feedback to create a testimonial and ask them to review and authorise it. Aim to create a one-page testimonial for every client engagement.

Now that you have a library of testimonials in place, it is time to write your biography. Why do you need this? You know the answer here: it establishes your credibility and helps you stand out from the crowd.

Make sure your biography contains your professional photograph and an introductory paragraph on who you are and what you do. Then add details about your relevant experience, qualifications and how to contact you. Ensure it's informative and succinct—try to keep it down to two pages. Keep it modern and professional-looking, don't add too many colours or graphics and aim to mimic the look of your website for consistency.

Step 4—Design A Logo

The last of the assumed credibility builders is your logo and business cards. This is what most new consultants and coaches do first—I guess it's the most fun. But too many of them go onto the internet, order a box of business cards and pick a cheesy logo that thousands of other people also use.

Designing a logo should be one of the last things you do. How can you design or have someone else design your company logo until you've finely tuned the services and benefits you offer, who they're aimed at and what you stand for? You can't. If you rush out and get a logo before doing the preparatory work above it will not represent you or your business. It won't be authentic.

Complete the brand-building steps in chapter one and create the other assumed credibility builders first. Take your time to settle on what you stand for and how you want the world to see you. Only then should you decide on your logo and get business cards printed.

When you design a logo or ask someone to design one for you, choose something that you have an emotional connection to. Make your logo something you're proud of and want to use everywhere. Then put it on your website, LinkedIn profile, letterheads, invoices, email footers and business cards. It might even be worth getting it embroidered onto your shirt.

You can get business cards incredibly cheaply, but they won't save you money in the long run. Choose high quality, but don't get too many printed at once. Due to social media and a decline in physical networking, people don't use business cards as much as they used to. If you order a large batch you'll have them for years, and you'll change branding before using them all.

There are some excellent providers out there that offer bespoke products with a luxury finish. However, stick to the basics: have your logo on the back and on the front have your company name, name, contact details and website address. Any other details are superfluous.

Step 5—Set Your Standards

The most obvious agreed credibility builders are the results and outcomes you write into your proposals. But there are two more. The first is your qualifications, knowledge and experience, and the second is the standard of service customers should expect when they work with you.

Having the relevant qualifications, knowledge and experience is essential. If you were an accountant, you'd be expected to have a degree in accountancy and be certified by the relative professional body. If you were a doctor, you'd also be expected to have the relevant qualifications.

What formal qualifications and certification do you need for your service? I have a master's degree in business administration (MBA), I'm a Fellow of the Institute of Sales Management (ISM) and I've coached some of the largest and most experienced consultancies. What's yours? For example, if you're a consultant who specialises in applying lean improvement within manufacturing organisations, you should probably have a degree in manufacturing management, a black belt in lean six sigma and perhaps ten years of working and training at Toyota.

If you want to establish your credibility and command high fees, you must be able to demonstrate your qualifications, knowledge and experience. If you already have the appropriate accolades, great—make sure they're on your personal biography. However, if you're missing one, two or all three of these, you need to enrol with the relevant organisations. Many universities offer distance learning and plenty of professional associations provide personal development. Investing in your qualifications and certifications now will give you more credibility in the future.

It's always good to set out your standards of service. Most large consultancies and professional service firms do this: they describe to the client what to expect and how you will treat them. However, most freelance consultants, trainers and advisors don't have these standards in place. This lack of standards is crazy as large firms already have a reputation for how they work with clients; you as an individual service professional don't. It's essential for potential clients who don't know you well to know what they can expect.

Clients want you to tell them these things before they commit because they want to feel reassured they'll be treated right. Here are the standards of service I use:

Effectiveness: I will always attend confirmed meetings and coaching sessions prepared and on time.

Ethics: I will always treat clients with respect, and I will always act in a professional manner.

Equality: I will always treat clients equally. I do not prioritise clients; no client is more important than another.

Efficiency: I will always make myself available for general communications as much as possible. If I am not able to talk to you, send an email or leave a phone message and I will reply within 24 hours.

Entrusted: I will always treat communications or information shared by a client with the utmost confidentiality. Nothing will be shared with others unless you give permission. I am happy to sign most non-disclosure agreements if requested.

I call this the '5E' service promise. What are your standards of service? Do you publicise them? Are they on your website? Do you tell clients about them before starting an assignment? If the answer is 'no' to any of these questions, I urge you to get them in place and use them.

Step 6—Go Beyond Expectations

Strictly speaking, you don't need to have delighted credibility builders in place—they're added extras—but it helps. Delighted credibility builders are the things clients don't ask for or expect but will be delighted with if they experience them. It's the small things that make a big difference, and this type of credibility builder moves you from good to great. Here are some examples of delighted credibility builders:

Handwritten notes

In a world of smartphones, emails and instant messaging, we've come to accept these as the default methods of written communication. In many cases, they've replaced verbal communication too. Sending a handwritten note with good old-fashioned pen and paper is now uncommon, yet it can be more personal and reassuring than the electronic alternative.

When was the last time someone went to the time and effort of sitting down and composing a handwritten note for you? Not to mention the inconvenience of buying a stamp and physically walking to a post box? Why would they do this when there are more convenient ways to send a message?

The answer is that writing a physical note shows they care

about you and want to demonstrate how important you are to them.

If a new client receives a handwritten note from you on some nice paper and written with a good pen, they'll be delighted. They'll know you care about them and value them. It can be as simple as writing a note to recognise a great coaching session, or to say you enjoyed meeting them and the stimulating conversation you had. Whatever the opportunity, use it to get some pen and paper and get writing.

Clients appreciate you saying 'thank you', and the best way to do this is through a handwritten note. In Dale Carnegie's book *How to Win Friends and Influence People*, he suggests some other helpful strategies:

- Become interested in other people
- Smile
- Remember that person's name
- Be a good listener
- Talk in terms of other people's interests
- Make other people feel important
- Thanking someone in a handwritten note incorporates all these points.

It's always good practice to thank clients for their business, and I don't just mean including a note at the bottom of your invoice. Take some advice from Dale Carnegie and make your client feel important. Send a handwritten note thanking them for choosing you and saying how much you're looking forward to working with them. Reassure the client they're going to achieve their goals. It always starts the assignment off on the right foot. You want your new clients to be talking to others about you in the most positive manner.

It's also worth sending a handwritten note partway through and after the assignment. This will keep the momentum up and finish the work on the best possible terms. It's also an excellent way to demonstrate how much you value the relationship, and will make clients more open to you asking for referrals.

A copy of your favourite book

Sending a book is a step up from sending handwritten notes. Write a message inside the book's cover to make it personal, then post your favourite book to someone you think might find it of interest and value. It costs money, so think about which book to send to that person. Even better, send them your own book. Writing and publishing a book is still something that most people don't do, but it's becoming more common to view it as an extended CV.

Whatever book you choose, send it with the genuine intention of adding value for the recipient, not to get a sale. They can tell the difference.

Personal confirmation of your meetings

Confirming your meetings in person is a small thing that takes a minute, but it can add another row of bricks to construct your credibility. It shows you're professional, organised, polite and prepared for the meeting—all characteristics clients look for in their coach or consultant.

Some people worry that sending a confirmation will make the client more likely to cancel the meeting. Maybe they're considering cancelling or postponing the meeting due to mounting demands on their time. But think about it: if you send a polite and professional confirmation reassuring that your session is important and valuable, which meeting will they decide to attend—the boring review meeting or the interesting one with the professional expert?

Another reason to send a confirmation is to make sure you don't turn up for the meeting and find out it's been cancelled. You'll have wasted a lot of time travelling and preparing for the session. By being professional and confirming beforehand, you protect your time. Besides, if a potential client cancels on the day of the meeting, they're not your ideal client anyway.

Step 7—Produce Recurring Materials

We've already created standard company materials like business cards that you can have to hand. These are your assumed credibility builders. But there's a second type of information materials we can use as delighted credibility builders. These are interesting and useful articles that are relevant to your target market.

When you write articles, ensure they add value for the reader and that they can look forward to reading them. Use them to highlight the challenges they face, the future direction of their sector and how you propose to address them. If you've done the work on building your brand in chapter one, you should already know what these are.

Recurring information materials can be produced in different formats. They might be a booklet, case studies or a podcast. Whatever form you choose, it's aim is to show your reader that you're an expert in your field, you have a great deal of knowledge of the sector, and you've helped lots of people just like them.

Create a series of articles so you can send or publish them regularly over a longish period. Then, when someone metaphorically raises their hand to let you know that your thoughts resonate with them, you can start a conversation.

Here's a sequence that will help you create recurring materials:

1. Write a series of articles
2. Make them interesting and informative
3. Send them out monthly
4. Start a conversation based on the article
5. Be ready to send a potential client your company brochure once they show interest in working with you

Don't forget to make your materials look modern and professional. Use MS Word to write and edit the content, then transfer it to some form of publishing software. There are lots of free, web-based options to help you create professional-looking documents. And don't forget to include your contact details and website address on everything you create.

You may think that writing consumes too much time or that you don't enjoy it. But having a library of information materials is one of those things that will set you apart from the crowd and, in turn, allow you to charge higher fees.

Photographs are an excellent addition to your articles, as they ramp up your credibility and likability even more. But while photographs are good, video is better. Reports highlight that compared to pictures, videos increase the consumer's purchase intent by 97% and brand association by 139%.

We know from a study conducted by Professor Mehrabian, Professor of Psychology at the University of California, that 7% of communication is verbal and 93% is non-verbal. In video, body language and verbal tone play a significant role in conveying your message, brand and credibility. Viewers can determine what you're trying to get across by observing how you hold yourself, how you speak and other visual clues. New clients want to get to know you before buying your services, as the very nature of coaching and consulting requires a great deal of trust. The more clients can see and listen to you, the more they'll get to know you, and the more at ease they'll be with starting a conversation.

A study found that consumers are 27 times more likely to click on an online video than a standard banner. Videos that have engaging content and a persuasive call to action do best at keeping their target market interested.

Videos are also more shareable. Few people would send a link to someone's photograph, but we all share videos as they're quick, concise and relatable—all the crucial elements of shareable content.

If you're still not convinced about video, look at the numbers. Social videos generate 1,200% more shares than images and text combined. And this number is only going to increase as video becomes more relevant.

However, in the same way that photographs must look professional, videos must be made and produced well. I see too many videos on LinkedIn and other platforms that look like the equivalent of holiday snaps.

Remember that you're aiming to establish yourself as an expert in your field—a likeable professional. No potential client is going to be convinced to use your services if you use an old iPhone to make a video of you sitting in your car. Videos like these look cheap, amateurish and self-indulgent.

Just like your article, your videos should be focused on your target market and provide them with new and useful information that's relevant to them.

Step 8—Raise Your Profile

There is a phrase, "People buy people". And it's true—your potential clients will want to hire you if they believe in you. One way to accelerate your credibility is to put yourself out there and become a more recognised public figure. This is challenging, but it's also one of the best ways to establish your credibility.

Think about it for a moment. Who are the most recognisable coaches and consultants in the market? Tony Robbins, Brian Tracey, Robin Sharma, Deepak Chopra, Michael Port, Martha Beck and Linda Basset are names that come to mind. You might know all, some or none of these names, but it doesn't matter. The point is that if you Google them you'll find page after page about them—articles, interviews, podcasts, news and talk show video clips on YouTube.

Most of your potential clients will not have heard of you. So make it easy for them to become aware of you and find out more from as many sources as possible.

If you're on TV or a newspaper or magazine runs an article on you, it gives your potential customer more evidence that you're a recognised expert. Real experts get that level of coverage, and experts have shorter sales cycles.

The more exposure you have, the more recognised you'll become within your target market. Potential clients will read, listen or watch to understand your approach and this will help them decide if they'd like to start a discussion. The bigger the queue of people wanting to engage in your services, the higher you can raise your fees.

So, get yourself out there. Get in front of the microphone, the camera, the podcast host or the journalist—anyone with a relevant audience—and start to gain instant credibility.

Step 9—Change Your Paradigms

The terms 'paradigm' and 'paradigm shift' were popularised through Thomas Kuhn's book *The Structure of Scientific Revolutions*. He described a paradigm as a system of rules and beliefs that we regard as established fact. So, a paradigm shift is when these rules are shown not to be true and we move from one set of rules to another.

It's not only scientists who have paradigms—they influence how we all see the world. We have paradigms on religion, relationships, ethics, everything—including selling consulting and coaching services.

Here are three paradigm shifts that could change how you go about getting clients.

Paradigm shift #1: Marketing does not get you clients

Before you slam this book down or throw it away, hear me out. Of course, marketing is a vital element of any business. But marketing alone will not get you a new assignment. You work within a high-trust service industry—if you post a marketing message on LinkedIn, nobody is going to read it and hire you. Trust and credibility need to be built beforehand.

Marketing creates awareness of your brand. It helps your target market understand who you work with and the benefits you help them achieve. It's the starting point of constructing your credibility. But it's what you do once a potential client becomes aware of you and has that first conversation that wins work. And the most important aspect of this is to help them walk through your sales cycle at a pace they are comfortable with.

Paradigm shift #2: Clients do not follow your sales cycle

Too many people think of selling professional services as a linear, step-by-step process. They think of it like pushing as many prospects as possible into a conceptual funnel. This funnel has a wide opening so they can stuff in thousands of people, then push them through the process until a few clients survive the ordeal and give them work.

The sales funnel has a fixed number of pre-defined steps where people are labelled and categorised. It couldn't be less like a personal service from a trusted expert who has a good relationship with their client. In fact, it looks and feels more like a sausage machine, churning and grinding people into similar products that will all be treated the same. That's not you and it's not what your clients want.

However, well-designed your sales funnel, your clients don't want to be forced to follow your process. They want to move at their own pace and take a unique route to work with you.

If somebody wants to buy your services, they don't want to be put through a 'validation' step and be classified as a 'lead'. Some will be naturally cautious and want to take their time before they buy. They don't want to be pushed before they're ready to jump. So, why would you waste your time and theirs writing a proposal before they're ready? Many service professionals do, in the hope of persuading someone to buy something they don't yet need or want. But it doesn't work.

All big corporations have a sales funnel to track and report the flow of potential clients. But these always have incorrect and missing information, which renders them useless, and CRM systems end up consuming a huge amount of effort for very little value. In any case, the sales team will manipulate the sales data consciously or unconsciously to present it in the best possible light. It's rare for a report from sales funnels to underestimate the potential value of work coming into the business.

Most people want to highlight the positives and conceal the negatives from their managers. This results in pushing clients through a process they're not ready for, and effort and money are wasted in providing an optimistic but inaccurate picture when they could have been focusing on attracting new clients.

Clients don't want to follow your process—they want to follow theirs. Your sales cycle needs to be adaptable for each person and their individual preferences. Of course, you need to monitor progress, but you should do this to support each person by providing the relevant information at the right time, allowing them to make the move of their own volition.

The sales cycle has one purpose and that's to construct credibility. It's not to sell. The minute you try to sell to someone who's not ready you'll lose potential clients. But if you focus on establishing yourself as an expert and a trusted adviser, the client will do all the sales work for you.

Change your business development model from a system that pushes people through a funnel to one where people can walk through themselves at a time and pace that suits them. This means that even those clients who weren't ready will come to you when their circumstances change and they need your help. All you have to do is provide everything they need to feel comfortable to ask for your support.

Think about that for a minute: you can create a sales cycle where the client comes to you. You are the expert, and it's you who decides if you work together, not them. Imagine how it feels to move from a push dynamic, where you force hundreds or thousands of prospects through a fixed process, to a pull dynamic where they're drawn to you.

Your sales cycle is there to construct credibility and build trust. When the time is right, potential clients will reach out, and when they do the sales conversation won't be "Convince me you can help', it'll be "Please can you do it".

Paradigm shift #3: You cannot sell coaching and consulting

No matter how good or detailed your sales cycle, a client will not buy your services if they don't need them. They need to find themselves in a situation that requires your support. As we discussed in chapter one, there are two reasons why someone buys consulting and coaching: fear and desire.

Clients need to be worried that something negative has happened or is about to take place. They will engage with you when they have a challenge they need to resolve or minimise. Alternatively, clients need to desire something positive in the future. They'll hire you when they want that ambition realised.

You can't sell to a client if everything is going well for them. If you try, it will make it hard to win work in the future when they do need your support. So, what's the solution? Design a sales cycle where you regularly keep in touch with potential clients. Focus on adding value, providing them with something of interest to construct your credibility. Make them aware of what you do and when the time is right, they'll reach out to you– when they need your help.

Your sales cycle should not be a well-oiled sales machine. It should be a garden where you sow seeds of credibility, then nurture them and watch them grow into strong, healthy trees. Do this and, nine times out of ten, you'll win the work when invited to a conversation.

Step 10—Design your sales cycle

We've already established that clients will hire credible experts when they need them, and that they'll want to do it their way. They need to consider you as trustworthy if they're to view you as a potential source of help.

You could design a complex, multi-layered sales cycle process, but in reality there are just three stages in the client's buying journey:

Awareness: Your target market gets to know and understand what you do and the benefits you bring.

Credibility: Your future client develops their trust in you and your service.

Decision: Your client considers you as the obvious choice when they need your help.

Each stage must be designed to increase your credibility and your potential client's trust in you. Sometimes these things can take a little time; most people do not buy on the first contact, although some do. We wouldn't expect to get married after a first date with someone, so why would we expect this to happen in sales? Just like romantic relationships, some sales happen quickly, while others take years.

This means that some of your clients will need a lot of tender loving care. Just as your level of commitment increases as a relationship develops, most clients will want to start small. You wouldn't give an engagement ring to someone you hardly knew, but you might give them flowers. Your purchases increase in proportion to the depth of the relationship and the growing level of trust. The same holds for business relationships. Most clients will want to buy small and increase the size of their purchases as your relationship and trust develop.

We're not alone in using this analogy. The sales coach Michael Port says that a sales cycle is like a love affair with your client and it should enable the client to progress smoothly from 'dating' to 'getting married'. A good way to do this is to offer four levels of service, each representing a different level of commitment. Then it's up to you and your client to agree on where to start and where to end up. The four levels are:

No hurdle (first date): This is the initial 'awareness' phase used to introduce yourself to your target market. Your offer should be free and so easy to consume and valuable that there's nothing to stop a client from saying "yes" to it. This offer shouldn't consume much of your time and should require minimal effort. Examples might include a free booklet you've written or a free webinar.

Low hurdle (boy/girlfriend): This is where the rubber hits the road. You offer something that doesn't cost the client much but delivers excellent value. This allows them to experience you and your services first-hand and with minimal risk. Examples of a low-hurdle offer might include a two-hour workshop or a one-day discovery review.

Medium hurdle (engaged): This is where strong, healthy relationships start. You've proven your services on a small scale and now it's time to offer a fuller service. This will require the client to make a more significant investment, but will be a small step if you've already provided some value. In return they get the benefits of the initial stages and will realise the positive outcomes to come if they proceed with a more extensive engagement.

High hurdle (married): By now you've built a good level of credibility, trust and even friendship with your client. It's time to put a full-service offering that requires a substantial investment on the table. If you've taken the time to walk the client through the no-, low- and medium hurdles and did an excellent job of it, you'll have constructed enough credibility for the client to feel comfortable committing to it.

So, let's summarise. At the start of your relationship with your client, offer something that presents no or little risk. Then, once you've got to know each other a little and have had an opportunity to demonstrate your potential value, the next time they reach out to ask for help, you can offer one of your more substantial services that correlate with your raised credibility.

Whether you adopt a four-stage or a ten-stage sales cycle, there are two simple questions you need to answer: What does my client want to do, and how am going to encourage them to do it? Look at it from their perspective, not yours.

Using an incremental and cumulative sales cycle creates a simple path for your clients to follow and constructs credibility, trust and healthy relationships. You'll bring an increased level of value to their lives, moving from the first date to married, where they'll buy your full service at top dollar. Remember: start small, prove your worth and end big.

❉ ❉ ❉

Ten Steps To Construct Credibility

Step 1—Get yourself sorted
Step 2—Establish your presence
Step 3—Create some material
Step 4—Design a logo
Step 5—Set high standards
Step 6—Go beyond expectations
Step 7—Produce recurring materials
Step 8—Raise your profile
Step 9—Change your paradigm
Step 10—Construct the cycle

POSITIONING PRICING

What

Understand your value, believe in yourself and ask for what you're worth. Then agree on a payment structure that's the best fit for you and the client.

Why

You want to make lots of money, while the client wants to feel they have a bargain. Follow this approach to position your pricing and achieve both outcomes.

How

Calculate the financial value you generate for your clients. Then set an attractive return on the client's investment to make it easy for the client to say "yes."

❊ ❊ ❊

In chapter one, Building Brands, we looked at how to categorise the benefits and outcomes of your work. I call these the five Es. If you haven't identified these, go back and complete that chapter before going any further. Your task now is to calculate the financial value of these benefits, so you can monetise the value your service provides. This is the first step in positioning pricing.

Step 1—Calculate Economic Outcomes

If the primary aim of your service is not financial, for example you're a life coach, you can skip this step. However, you should still look to monetise the benefits captured by the four remaining Es, so keep reading this chapter.

This step is for businesses where the primary benefit of the service is financial. This benefit can be one of two things: an outcome that generates more revenue or an outcome that improves liquidity, i.e. profit and cash flow.

Each of these outcomes can also be broken down into two. You can generate more revenue by either reducing costs or by increasing the money coming in, and you can increase liquidity either by reducing the value of fixed assets and liabilities or by increasing the money coming in.

If your service's primary purpose is to produce a financial benefit, you should understand the pyramid of financial ratios. You should also be familiar with terms such as 'return of total assets' (ROTA), 'return on sales' (ROS) and 'asset utilisation ratio' (AUR). If you don't, I recommend you study *Key Management Ratios* by Ciaran Walsh. It's a go-to book for me when I work with a company's board or financial director.

So, what are the direct financial benefits your client can expect from your work? Is it a 20% reduction in costs? Or a 15% increase in sales? Or, even better, is it a combination of reduced costs and increased revenue? Perhaps your primary output is to improve cash flow by increasing stock turns, and you aim to achieve this by reducing inventory.

Whatever the primary output of the project, your client will have already quantified the obvious top-level benefits before your first conversation. If you haven't done your homework beforehand to get a rough understanding of their financial performance, you're behind their curve.

Step 2—Monetise Effectiveness Outcomes

This is about improving the quality of your client's product or service—helping them do things right first time to the standard expected of their customers. Its primary financial impact is to increase profit.

Effectiveness outcomes might involve work tasks, processes, data or increasing employee productivity or dependability. Perhaps part of the remit is to reduce the rate of defective products within a manufacturing process. Or it might be to alter a call centre system to increase customer retention.

Or you might be a career coach who works with individuals to help them return to work. In this case, you'd seek to understand how the client's challenges are affecting their financial position. Perhaps a person's situation is stopping or reducing their ability to work and earn money. What was their salary before? What could it be if they recovered? In this example, your primary benefit would be to get your client back to work, and the financial outcome of doing this would be a salary of £20,000.

Effectiveness can generate both cost-saving and revenue benefits. How much more money will this create for your clients?

Step 3—Monetise Efficiency Outcomes

Efficiency outcomes are about speed. If your client has elements in their life or business that aren't flowing quickly and smoothly, they'll be losing money. The primary effect of an efficiency benefit is to improve cashflow.

Let's imagine one of your clients is a florist who delivers

flowers two days from the point of order. How many more sales could they generate if you helped them to offer same-day deliveries? They'd be making more revenue while keeping their fixed costs the same.

Or perhaps you have a client who takes three days to approve a request from a different part of their company. Time is money, and most of this processing time is lost with items sitting around not being used. Streamlining the client's process would improve how they utilise their assets.

Step 4—Monetise Emotional Outcomes

This is all about emotional connections, like a company's staff engagement or an individual's state of mind. Are the client's staff engaged with the organisation's mission? You might not think you can find financial benefits here, but dig a little deeper and you might find hidden costs.

Poor engagement can lead to low employee retention rates. In fact, a recent study put the average cost of losing an employee and recruiting a replacement at £30,000. If you can improve employee engagement and the staff's connection with the company, that might result in fewer people leaving. And improving the emotional wellbeing of employees could also raise their performance, increase their productivity and reduce time lost to sickness.

If you're working with an individual rather than a company, the critical question to ask is: "How are this person's emotional challenges costing them money?" You'll need to have a sensitive discussion with them to understand their situation and the adverse financial outcomes.

Step 5—Monetise Environment Outcomes

This is about focusing on a client's physical work environment. It is well established that improving the workplace can benefit the organisation and its employees. Are items being moved about too much due to a lousy layout causing wasteful activity? Has a poorly located filing cabinet caused an injury and time off work? Or has poor lighting caused a production operative not to see a defect? The list is endless.

You might be a *feng shui* expert who improves the aura of people's houses. I know of one who helps clients who have trouble selling their homes, and most of her clients sell within a few weeks of the consultation. Her fees are up to £5,000 for a two-hour session, which is great money for her and a fraction of the value of her clients' £1 million houses. Her offer, at its most simplistic level, is "You give me £5,000 and I'll help you get £1,000,000." It's a good deal for both the consultant and the client.

Step 6—Calculate Client ROI

Most consultants and coaches approach pricing by scanning their competition to establish the going market rate and then setting their fees at a similar level. But your price should be set by the value you generate, not what your competitors charge.

The conversation takes a different path if you can make an offer to a client that provides a good return on their investment. Then the discussion will centre on the value you generate rather than entering a negotiation based on price alone.

The saying 'you get what you pay for' is as valid for consulting and coaching as anything else. If your prices are high, it's worth highlighting to a client that the reason you're expensive is that you generate more benefit than others in your field. Do they want to save small or gain more substantial benefit? If their answer is to save small, they're not the right client for you.

You should be able to quantify the overall return on your client's investment (ROI) once the outputs of your work have been monetised. Then you can decide how much you will charge.

Again, I understand that financial gain might not be the primary aim of your service, but even so your clients will want to justify the investment to themselves or others. In short, it must make sound financial sense to hire you. Your client might tell you that they're not interested in the economic benefit, but I guarantee that someone else will be. That could be the financial director, other stakeholders in the company, or even the client's spouse.

Your services should produce an ROI of at least four times more than they cost. This is the minimum—most clients look for an ROI of ten or higher. If you could estimate that your services would generate an ROI of 100, who would turn down that offer?

Step 7—Invoice after work

The first question you should ask yourself when you invoice for your work is: "When do I want to get paid?" There are three possible answers: after you've done the work, during the project, or before you start. Most people would like to be paid beforehand, but very few are. A client will ask themselves the opposite question: "When is the latest I can pay?" While you want a quick payment, they'll want to pay as late as possible.

Why do you allow yourself to be in this situation? The payment structure you adopt will hinge on one thing: how much credibility you have constructed. Do your clients believe you have the ability to help them achieve their goals? Have you taken the time to present yourself as a trusted, credible, professional and likeable expert in your field? If you have, the client will feel more at ease with paying before work starts to secure your services. On the other hand, if there are questions about your abilities, the client will look to offset the perceived risk. They will look to pay after, or at best during the assignment.

The level of credibility you construct will determine where the balance of power sits. If you're a sought-after expert, you hold the power. Conversely, if the client considers you to be just one of many providing a similar service, the power will be theirs.

Money for time

The most common approach to charging is invoicing the client for the time you've spent on their project. You send a client an invoice at the end of the month, and they pay 30 days after receiving it. But think about it: that often means you don't get paid until 60 days after giving them your valuable time.

This approach opens you up to risk. What happens if the client refuses or is unable to pay? They might use a minor detail as an excuse to avoid paying you to boost their profits. You'll then be forced to take legal action, which costs you time and money and could result in the client attempting to ruin your reputation.

Why do so many coaches and consultants allow themselves to end up in this situation? The answer is because the client holds the balance of purchasing power. And why is this? Because you didn't take the time to establish yourself as a specialist and build demand for your services.

Money for achievement

In this charging model, your fees are dependent on achieving a pre-agreed level of performance or progress. It's suitable for projects with a defined start and finish date and tangible outputs.

The money for achievement payment structure often comes in two parts: a small monthly payment to cover your expenses and a second, large payment made after achieving a specified result. A simple example would be where you agree to a monthly subsistence fee of £1,000 followed by a performance payment of £70,000 for achieving a specified milestone. This amount can be substantial if it's linked to an output that has a higher value for the client, but you must have agreed conditions to confirm if it's been achieved.

Like money for time, money for achievement involves most of your fees being paid after the work. The offset is that you can charge a higher price than usual, but it still means you taking much of the risk.

Step 8—Invoice During Work

If you've constructed a good level of credibility and likeability, you may be able to charge your clients during the work. One option is for the client to sign up to a 'pay as you go' subscription contract.

Money for subscription

The subscription model is useful when the client wants access to your services but doesn't have the funds to pay for it in a single payment. To work out what they should pay, calculate the value of your service and then break it down into smaller regular payments, for example, offer a 12-week subscription at £100 per week instead of £1,200 all at once. Subscriptions bring balance to who holds the power. If you keep providing excellent service, the client continues to pay; if your standards slip, the client can cancel the subscription.

Subscriptions are reactive; if a client stops paying, you stop providing the service, reducing the potential amount of money lost. Of course, there is still a level of risk. A client could lose their commitment or enthusiasm for the work and drop the subscription. Your losses are limited, but you'll still need to expend time and effort to enrol a new client sooner than expected. If you notice a number of clients cancelling their subscription, it's a good indication your services need to improve.

Step 9—Invoice Before Work

Most of us want to be paid before starting work, and clients will tolerate advance payment if you've built the right level of credibility. If the client trusts you, they'll consider the engagement as a low-risk purchase.

There are two main payment structures that enable you to be paid before work starts: money for access and money for product.

Money for access

Sometimes a client who respects and values your advice is happy to pay in advance to secure a prioritised direct 'hotline' to you. For example, when someone is arrested and they say, "Get my lawyer", it means they've paid a retainer to ensure the lawyer can be called on in times of need.

A model where people pay in advance to secure your time represents the highest level of trust. It can be very lucrative, as the client pays in advance for your service irrespective of if they use it. But if a client paying a retainer calls on you, you need to respond to support your client right away. Therefore, you need to retain enough free capacity to provide the service at short notice.

Only offer a retainer service to one or two clients at most. Otherwise you risk a situation where more than one retainer client needs your help at the same time. To avoid potential misunderstandings it's also wise to stipulate a service level agreement, the primary condition being what your response time will be.

Money for product

A 'product' doesn't have to be physical. It can be a fixed-price standard service that delivers repeatable outcomes. Here, you distil your years of experience to design a standard process that all your clients follow.

To productise your service, you need to create a methodology that is robust enough to generate excellent outcomes but flexible enough to accommodate different clients' requirements. The product should consume the same amount of your time irrespective of the assignment. This makes it easy to set a standard price and produce a consistent profit.

An example of this is a management consultant conducting a diagnostic project to identify a client's losses of productivity. The consultant knows that it always takes five working days to gather and analyse the data and another five to define the improvement opportunities and write a report.

They know the analytical techniques and the data required, although the activities to capture the data might vary from client to client. They also know that, no matter where the client's data is, nine times out of ten it can be retrieved within two or three days.

In this example, the consultant can offer a diagnostic 'product' with a fixed price of £20,000. This equates to £2,000 per day minus expenses, coming out at a net £1,500 per day.

The combination of a standard price and consistent costs and processes allow you to charge before work starts. Both you and the client know what is entailed and, of course, being paid beforehand eliminates the payment risk.

Step 10—Consider Offering Discounts

Another question to ask yourself is: "Am I willing to reduce my prices to get more clients?". There will be times when you consider lowering your fees, for example if you don't have enough clients and would like more. Another time you might do this is if there is a specific client who you especially want to work with. In these cases, you might be willing to sacrifice a little profit for the opportunity to work with this person.

Irrespective of the discount approach you adopt, it must be made clear to clients when the offer is valid and when the standard prices resume. Don't allow your discounted rates to be in place too long—otherwise they'll be considered as your standard price.

There are a few options open to you:

Discount for bundling

This involves combining two or more distinct services into a single 'bundled' offering. The bundle is better value than if they were to be bought separately. One of the most recognised practitioners of this approach is the fast-food chain McDonald's. It used to structure its menu by listing all the individual items and customers ordered their food by picking whichever burger, fries, drink and ice cream they wanted.

McDonald's realised they could make the customer experience easier and sell more products by bundling them together. Their 'value meals' were priced lower than if the customer were to buy each individual item, and the combination of value to the customer and ease of ordering make the bundled meals the most popular option to this day.

This approach doesn't just work with fast food chains. It can work with coaching and consulting services, too. For example, you might offer clients four services—let's call them 'Bronze', 'Silver', 'Gold' and 'Platinum'—each increasing in value from the previous one:

Bronze = £1,000
Silver = £3,000
Gold = £9,000
Platinum = £15,000

Clients can buy one service alone, or they can buy a combined service of Bronze and Silver together at a cheaper rate, providing more value for you and for the client. Both of you get more for less—a rare win-win situation. The client gets more services for less money, and you get more revenue for less marketing.

When marketing bundled services, it's essential to highlight the additional value the client gets by buying them together. Make it clear this is a limited offer, for example, clients cannot buy the Bronze service and then return a few months later to buy the Silver service at the discounted price.

If you're tempted to allow this, think about the mayhem that would ensue if McDonald's did this for its customers. Imagine someone buying a burger, then returning ten minutes later to order fries and a drink, asking for a value meal discount to be applied retrospectively. They wouldn't accept it, and neither would the other customers who had paid full price. Make your bundle discount offer at the start of the relationship and withdraw it if not taken up by the customer.

Discount for volume

This discounting model involves offering to reduce your fees in exchange for more work. Volume discounting is different from bundling. A volume discount is providing more of the same service, whereas bundle discounts offer a collection of services.

In the previous McDonald's example, bundling is taking the individual items and combining them into a single value meal. Volume discounting would equate to the size of the meal—standard, large or supersize. So instead of offering two portions of fries for £2.00, you'd offer one supersize portion for £1.50.

If you're running a workshop, one of the best ways to make more money is to charge per person rather than charging for your time. For example, if your standard approach is to run a two-day workshop for ten people charged at £100 per head, you might decide to offer a client the same workshop for 15 participants at a discounted rate of £80 per head. It's the same two days of work for you but with 20% more revenue. And the client is happy because they get a 20% reduction. Every supermarket employs this method to sell more: four for the price of three, buy two get the third half-price, etc.

Another example could involve a 'time for money' quote

that is discounted if the client wants to extend. For example, you might charge £120,000 for an assignment based on £2,000 per day over 60 days. If you like the client and have no other work in the pipeline, it could make good business sense to offer a discount for an additional 30 days support. This way, you can keep money coming in while you look for your next client.

Discount for demand

You might think that seasonal demand applies only to retail, but it's relevant to coaches and consultants, too. Just as clothing shops discount products before the new season arrives when few people are buying them and train companies charge less if you travel off-peak, you too can discount when things are quiet and raise prices at busy times. The key is to understand when your clients use your services.

Demand varies for consulting and coaching, and it often follows budgeting cycles and the holiday seasons. Work tends to roll in once budgets have been approved in April, after which demand tends to decrease during popular vacation periods as companies delay the start of a project until their employees return.

Ask yourself: "When are my busiest and quietest times?" When demand is high, keep your fees high; conversely, when demand is low consider discounting your prices to keep your paid utilisation high.

Discount for entry

This strategy is about encouraging clients to try your services by setting fees low for a limited time. You use that time to work hard and build credibility with the client and then raise your prices once a strong, trusting relationship is established.

This is akin to the 'loss leader' approach often used when selling physical products. For example, new entrants in the automotive sector often set low prices for their cars to encourage people to buy their products. The carmaker often makes a loss in the short term but has a longer-term strategy of raising prices once the reputation of the car is more established. Skoda, Hyundai and Kia all did it—they sold cars below the market standard before raising them when their popularity grew. Skoda entered the UK market selling cars for less than £6,000; now they sell their vehicles above £40,000. Dacia is the current new entrant and is adopting the same strategy, selling small cars for less than £7,000 when the average price is £15,000.

Other products do this too: they sell the first item at a loss but make subsequent purchases more expensive. Printers are cheap to buy, but the replacement ink cartridges are costly. Razors are inexpensive, but the replacement blades are sold at extraordinary prices.

You can apply this approach to coaching and consulting too, but it can be risky. You could reduce your fees because you consider yourself as a new entrant or you want to use an untested service, adopting a strategy of starting cheap and raising prices once you're established. The problem is that clients will expect you to keep your process low. People who buy cheap tend to shop around for the best deal. They're not too interested in building a long-term relationship—they tend to view business as transactional.

Make clear from the outset that the initial period is discounted. Tell the client what your standard fees are and when they will start to apply. Whenever you take on a new client using this approach, ensure the proposal sets out both the discounted and standard fees.

For example, your proposal might state that the assignment lasts 30 working days. The cost of the first five days is cut by 50%, but the standard fees apply to the subsequent 25. If the client is still nervous, you might offer to hold a review after the first five days. At this point, the client has the option to stop the assignment or continue at the standard rates. Whatever you do, the proposal must make clear the quantity of discounted days or hours and when your fees revert to the standard rates.

Discount for payment

If your cash flow situation is tight, discount for payment is an option worth considering. This is where you offer a discount if a client pays a proportion of your fees in advance. This discounting approach allows you to adopt the 'money for time' payment structure but also integrate an advance payment to offset the risk.

Offer a small discount but set it higher than the interest rates available from banks. Then, if a client has a good level of liquidity, they could be tempted to pay a proportion beforehand for a discount.

The advice I give to all my clients is to keep the payment structure simple. Offer a straightforward trade—you give me X and I give you Y. Complex payment structures and discounts tend to increase the potential for disagreements and can cause withheld payments and troubled relationships.

Above all remember this: credible experts—the people who help clients achieve extraordinary results—are busy. They don't need to discount their fees to get a new client. Cutting your prices might give the impression of inexperience, so use discounts with care.

* * *

Ten Steps To Position Your Pricing

Step 1—Calculate economy outcomes
Step 2—Monetise effectiveness outcomes
Step 3—Monetise efficiency outcomes
Step 4—Monetise emotional outcomes
Step 5—Monetise environment outcomes
Step 6—Calculate client ROI
Step 7—Invoice after work

Step 8—Invoice during work
Step 9—Invoice before payment
Step 10—Consider offering discounts

MANAGING MARKETING

What

Marketing is the recurring activities you perform to promote you and your services. Tell your target market who you are, what you do, and the benefits you provide.

Why

Marketing does not get you work—its purpose is to start a dialogue with potential clients. It's the fuel of constructing credibility that creates momentum to start conversations.

How

Build deeper relations with existing contacts, expand your network and get introduced to more people who are relevant to your business.

※ ※ ※

In Chet Holmes's book *The Ultimate Sales Machine*, he estimates that just 2–3% of people in any given target market are ready to buy your services. A further 6–7% are open to the idea of using your services, and 30% know they need help but are not ready to explore options for support.

That means around 60% of your target market do not believe they have a problem and are not even considering using services like yours. In my experience, you can group this target market population into three groups:

Shoppers: 8% to 10% looking to buy your services

Searchers: 20% to 30% thinking about whether they need support

Snubbers: 60% to 70% not wanting help at all

These numbers mean that most people in your sector do not want to receive any form of sales message, but will be happy to receive useful information that's of interest to them.

There are lots of different ways to promote your services, some good and others not so good. Above all, remember: you are a service professional who is aiming to create a meaningful relationship with clients.

Let's get one thing straight from the outset. Radio, newspaper and magazine adverts are useless. They cost a fortune and people forget them. I've found that paying for marketing campaigns on social media doesn't produce the outcomes hoped for either, and they too can be expensive. In my opinion, these are not the right approaches for people selling professional services like you and me.

You are looking for clients, not customers. It's a different relationship. Customers buy products, while clients invest in experts to provide help and advice. It costs roughly £3,000 to run a 30-second advert on a local radio station late at night when there are few listeners. You'll be paying £10 per second to advertise to people who aren't interested. Keep your money and build your reputation through a more personal approach instead.

If you want people to consume your promotional materials,

make them about your target market, not about you. Remember that the primary purpose of marketing professional 'high-trust' services is to construct your credibility and position yourself as the go-to person with a specific skill set. Only a small amount of effort should go into letting people know how great you are.

Step 1—Focus Your Marketing

We've talked about how important it is to define your target market and your model clients. To design and implement a successful promotional campaign, you need to focus your efforts on your target market once again.

Marketing a physical product is like fishing using a trawler with a large net. It scoops up everything in its way—relevant or not. Marketing consulting and coaching is more like fishing with a rod and line. It brings in a few big fish, but only of the type the fisherman is interested in. The trawler is expensive; the rod and line are not.

Focus your marketing efforts on your target market and don't be tempted to spend a lot of money promoting to people who aren't relevant. Your marketing strategy should be to construct credibility that leads to conversations. To do that, it needs to be fit for use. If you open a dictionary and flick through the letter 'R', it will contain all the words that are important to marketing:

Relevance: having a direct bearing on the matter in hand (your target market)

Results: creating a valuable outcome by solving a problem (your benefits)

Respect: showing you as polite and considerate (your model client)

Reputation: making you well known, so that others hold a high opinion of you (your future clients)

Relationships: being connected or related to you (your clients)

Rapport: a sympathetic relationship or understanding (you appreciate their challenges and ambitions)

Realism: being pragmatic rather than holding a moral or dogmatic view (your approach)

Reflectiveness: being careful and considerate (your mindset)

Regularity: occurring at a fixed or prearranged interval (your monthly contact with clients)

Relatability: establishing an association between people (you and your target market)

Resonance: a sound produced in sympathy with a neighbouring source (your client thinks as you do)

Responsiveness: reacting or replying to something (your client asking for a conversation)

Revelation: being significant and important

Rewards: being gratifying and giving satisfaction

I'm sure that if I flicked through the dictionary again, I'd find more 'Rs' that are relevant to marketing consulting and coaching, but for now pick five—or use all of them. This is Be Yourself Sales after all. You decide what works for you.

The important point is to determine which of the 'Rs' appeal to you most and use these as a checklist before sending out any marketing materials.

Step 2—Create Marketing Materials

In chapter two, Constructing Credibility, I stated that you need to create two sets of information material: a company brochure with one-page overviews for each service you provide and a series of interesting and informative articles, videos or podcasts that are relevant to your target market.

Your marketing effort should follow the 80/20 rule, where 80% focuses on constructing your credibility and the remaining 20% is used to promote your services. This is because your messages need to be welcomed by the people you are contacting. The more relevant and helpful they are, the more your audience will pay attention. If you send bland, boring or irrelevant materials that add no value, they'll consider you a nuisance and think of you as a 'spammer'. Marketing is not about you, it's about them.

All the marketing materials you create should be provided free, and most shouldn't contain a sales message at all. Let me say that again: most of your marketing should not be an attempt to sell. It's to build your credibility and to establish yourself as an expert in your field.

No matter how impressive your marketing is, if people don't need your support, they won't buy. Marketing is a long game—it's to make sure that you're at the front of a client's mind when their situation changes and they do need help. You can't force them to buy, but you can be there for them when they need you.

Done well, marketing constructs your credibility so that, when the time is right, clients will come to you and start a conversation. You hold the sales power; you've created the demand for your services.

When you have a sales conversation at the right time, it focuses on the positive aspects of how you help the client. That's a different starting point from your competitors. You're already two steps ahead of them.

While the majority (80%) of your marketing materials should be focused on your target market's situation, you do need to promote your services and tell people about what you do. This is where the remaining 20% of your marketing comes into play. Use your brochure and one-page service overviews to inform clients what you do and the benefits you bring. The 20% should also include items that bring colour and vitality to what you offer. These might include:

Situations clients might find themselves in (to demonstrate when to contact you)

Case studies of successful, relevant assignments (to prove you have a track record of working with people like them)

New services (to offer a solution for an emerging challenge within their sector)

Whatever format you use to promote your services, it must be structured to grab people's interest and entice them to consume what you provide.

Step 3—Connect With Friends

You need to build your potential client's trust in you before holding a sales conversation; faith is not established overnight. Few people will offer an assignment after one email or a single article, so don't expect to land a client after one interaction. You need to connect with people regularly. The aim of 'connecting' marketing activity is to develop meaningful, deeper and stronger relationships with individuals you already know.

They could be previous or current clients, old colleagues, friends, or that pesky potential client who you've never managed to work with. These people should be within your target market, and their personalities and characteristics should align with your model client criteria.

If you split your time equally between connecting with clients and colleagues, everybody wins. A lot of your business will come from other service professionals, as they may offer something different than you. As a result, they'll be happy to refer business to you or to work together on an assignment in partnership.

When you send a message to someone within your network, make it personal. Don't use the same email template for everyone as they'll know what you've done and it sticks out a mile. Use your email to share where you are, what you're working on or even how you feel—you know these people, after all. Keep it informal, short and to the point. Here's a suitable example:

Hi Max

I was driving down the M5 motorway past your office, and it reminded me of the project we worked on last year. So, I thought I would drop a note to say 'hi.'

You know how every now and then I write articles? Well, here's one I wrote about the success factors of implementing change in a call centre. Let me know what you think about it.

Thanks, Peter

Five crucial elements of this email are:
1. It's short
2. It's personal
3. It provides something of value
4. It contains an invitation to respond, and
5. It's not trying to sell or promote anything.

You don't need to get drawn into mass marketing. I've found that, to build a healthy and sustainable revenue, you should be connected to just 80 relevant people. I call this your 'group of 80', and you should stay in touch with them monthly. "80 every month! How much time do you think I have?" you might think. But it's not that much work when you break it down.

There are 20 working days in a month, which works out as four people a day. It takes two or three minutes to write an email, so if you stay focused, your connection marketing will consume just ten to fifteen minutes a day. You could even do it when having breakfast before your workday starts.

Monthly contact with people you know could produce four or five large assignments, which I'm sure you'd agree is a good return on your 15 minutes a day investment.

In summary, say 'hi' and send some useful information to four people you already know in your target market each day. Don't try to sell to them. When they need you, they'll ask for a conversation because you've reminded them that you're friends and you can help them with the challenges they face.

Step 4—Meet New People

Networking, on first impressions, might seem like an extension of the connection approach, but it's actually quite different. Connection marketing is about developing deeper relationships with people you know; networking is all about meeting and getting to know new people.

The 80/20 rule is a recurring theme in marketing, and just as I've said that you should stay in contact with 80 existing connections, you should try to create a 'roll of 20' people you want to meet for the first time. These are people in your target market who either might become clients or could introduce you to potential clients.

Formal networking events work better for coaches than consultants, as coaches tend to work on a one-to-one or small group basis. Consultants are more likely to work with companies, and not many large companies attend this type of meeting.

A good networking group will meet weekly. Attendees should come from a range of professions to avoid friction between competitors. A diverse community will encourage an environment where relationships are established and referrals flow.

You should consider joining a formal networking group if you're a coach and your group of 80 or list of 20 isn't yet populated. Here are a few pointers for when you attend a formal networking event or any other activity that presents a networking opportunity:

Be smart: Set out beforehand what you want to achieve. What would need to happen for you to leave the event feeling you've had a productive evening? Set some targets; how many people you'll meet, how many follow up meetings you'll arrange and how many business cards you'll hand out and receive. I'm not the most sociable person, so I tend to leave the event as soon as I've hit my targets, but if you enjoy socialising then stay as long as you like—whatever suits you most.

Be prepared: Too many people ramble on at networking events until the other person becomes bored and excuses themselves in a bid to escape. To make sure you're not one of these bores, spend time preparing in advance. Go back to chapter one and re-read how to talk about yourself, then practise what you're going to say in a safe environment, perhaps with family or friends.

Be selfless: If you're trying to build a long-lasting rapport with people in your target market, nothing beats unsolicited generosity. Stand out from everyone else in the room by offering them the free, no-risk option you set in the initial stages of your sales cycle, for example inviting them to dial into one of your webinars. Offer something of value with no obligation. Empathy surpasses selling in networking events, so make every effort to use your experience and expertise to help others and they'll come back asking for more.

Be interested: Ask questions and make every effort to concentrate when listening to their answer. You might find common subjects to talk about, or you might find they have a challenge or ambition you can help with. If you have a good conversation, you might feel comfortable enough to ask if they would like to meet afterwards to continue it.

Be personable: The easiest way to build trust at a business gathering is by getting personal. It's a natural human trait that individuals want to work with people they like—your ideal client. Keep the discussion light, fun and engaging. Concentrate on making acquaintances first and business connections second. Potential clients don't like pretence and, while you don't need to become best friends, the best deals are struck when you keep it professional and authentic.

Be authentic: Have in mind the characteristics of your model client. Talk to people who match your criteria and who are interested in you. Don't try to be someone you're not if you're aiming to meet this person again. It could cause future problems as you can't pretend to be somebody else forever.

Be patient: How many times have you been given a business card and put it straight in the bin when you get home? No one wants a business card they haven't asked for, so don't shove your business cards into people's hands. Wait until they offer their card or ask them for it—this puts you in control of the follow-up.

Be responsive: The conversations you have at these events are just the starting point of a more extended discussion, so don't be content with hoarding business cards. Follow up to establish lines of communication within 24 hours of meeting them. Scientists have found that we tend to forget information we don't engage with repeatedly. In fact, if two days pass before reviewing information, we forget 60% of what was said. This is called the 'forgetting curve'.

Contacting someone the day after you meet them demonstrates that you want an authentic business relationship, but make sure you check with them how they'd like to stay in touch. The longer you leave it the more they'll forget, and if you don't follow up at all you'll have spent a day at a networking event that you'll never get back.

Step 5—Network Through Linkedin

Social media has evolved to become an essential element of marketing. It works because, as with webinars, social media allows two-way communication. The clue is in its name: 'social'. Compared with traditional, outbound communication methods, it's much easier to build lasting relationships.

LinkedIn is a particularly useful platform to find new clients and promote your services as its users' number in the hundreds of millions spread over hundreds of countries. Its mission statement is to "connect the world's professionals to make them more productive and successful."

You might have joined LinkedIn because it felt like a good thing to do, or maybe your colleagues are members, but you might not have given much thought to how to use it as a business development tool.

When you use a social media platform like LinkedIn, ask yourself this question: "If this was a face-to-face meeting, what would I say and do?" For example, when you meet someone for the first time, would you introduce yourself as a "high-powered super serial entrepreneur who delivers high ROIs with low CPUs while maximising IQs"? I thought not. It might sound impressive, but in reality it smacks of a severe lack of confidence or an inflated ego. Either way, you wouldn't want to hire this person.

How many times have you accepted a connection request on LinkedIn and then received a long message from them trying to punt their services? Too often. When that happens I disconnect immediately, and I'm not the only one who does this. Unsolicited messages that contain a sales pitch won't get you anywhere. This includes posting self-promotional comments to other people's LinkedIn posts. You'll be consigned to the spam folder and the connection deleted.

If you use it correctly, LinkedIn has excellent business development potential, but many users get stuck pushing out one-way posts. They talk but don't listen, post but don't interact, shout and ignore.

Face to face, these approaches do not work. Can you imagine attending a networking meeting and behaving like this? It would be chaos: 100 people all shouting at each other about how great they are, bragging about the awards they've won and showing photographs of their swanky new office.

I'm pretty sure you wouldn't attend a meeting like that again. So, treat LinkedIn like any kind of networking: engage people in conversation, interact and share relevant, interesting information. This is the best way to build trust, establish credibility and start a conversation that leads to an authentic professional relationship.

When you're in a meeting, everything you say, do and present reflects on you and your business. The same applies to the way you interact with others on LinkedIn, so be careful what you comment on other people's posts. Everything you say and do in the virtual world should mirror how you behave in the real world.

Treat direct messages on LinkedIn the same as if you were talking to a person in real life, too. What would you do if you met someone at an event and had this conversation?

You: "Hi, I'm Isla, nice to meet you."
Jo: "Hi, Isla, I'm Jo, would you like to buy my services?"

You'd think it was weird, right? If your sales approach is to send lots of information with a strong sales message straight after connecting with someone, stop. It makes you look stupid or desperate—or both.

Do lots of networking, but do it in a thoughtful and considerate fashion. Communicate to each person in a unique way that's relatable and respectful. That way, you'll be viewed as someone worth replying to.

When you send a connection request on LinkedIn, first ask yourself why you want to do so. Make sure you have a genuine reason for contacting them, then tell the person you're reaching out to who you are, what you do and why you'd like to connect. People don't want to spend time trying to figure it out.

Include a personal message to show you're not using a formatted template or automated robot. Demonstrate that you know some of their work and like their approach. Reassure them that you're not asking for anything—you're just introducing yourself. As with all electronic messages, it should be short and to the point. Here's an example:

Hi Lisa,

My name is Peter Brodie and I'm a sales coach for consultants and coaches.

I was flicking through LinkedIn and came across an article you posted. It was on the importance of coaching team members rather than telling them what to do. It resonated with me; it's nice to read another's thoughts that align with your own.

Thanks for the article, it was thoughtful and well written.

I have written a similar report that raises a few other points; please do let me know if you would like to read it and I'll send it over.

Sincerely,
Peter Brodie

There are some elements in this message worth highlighting:

It's short, so there's a good chance the recipient will read it.

I'm not trying to sell anything.

I let her know who I am and what I do.

I compliment her work and highlight that we think the same way.

I finish by offering something of value with no assumptions and without asking for anything in return.

Given time and a few more valuable communications, this person might grow to appreciate your contributions. This is your opportunity to construct your credibility. When the time is right for them, they'll initiate a business conversation to find out more about you.

A little bit of preparation can go a long way, so do some research to find common interests and talking points. For example, you could:

Identify this person's colleagues. Do you have a mutual acquaintance or friend in common? Don't assume that shared connections on LinkedIn are genuine; many people are connected but don't know each other.

Find out if there are hobbies or interest you share. Is there something topical happening that you're both aware of?

Establish if you worked in the same or similar organisations, or perhaps their competition. Demonstrate you understand their challenges and ambitions.

Know if you could help this person. What is unique and special about you that makes it obvious you should work together?

Just as with maintaining your connections, aim to establish a regular tempo for your networking activities. Try to contact all the people in your roll of 20 once a month—that equates to one person per workday. Keep in regular contact with them, add value and don't try to sell them anything.

Step 6—Ask For Referrals

Getting and giving referrals can be tricky and it needs to be approached with care. After all, reputations are on the line. References are the most effective and efficient way to get more clients, but people will only refer you to others if you've done an excellent job for them.

One of the reasons I encourage everyone to identify and work with model clients is that this is when you do your best work. And you want people talking about your best work, don't you? You would never ask for a referral if you knew in your heart that you'd done an average or poor job.

The power of referrals means there's no need to spend money on LinkedIn advertising or Google ads. Let your happy clients spread the word for you. If you do it well, your rate of referrals can accelerate dramatically, as one client might refer two new clients, and these two refer four clients, and so on.

But if your work didn't satisfy your client's expectations, this multiplication effect could have negative consequences. Most of the studies on customer satisfaction agree that around 85% of dissatisfied customers will tell between nine and eighteen other people about the bad experience. The remaining 15% will tell more than 20 people. That's why, in the long run, it's imperative you choose your clients with care.

Referrals come with a level of indirect sales burden, and most of your clients and partners are not experienced salespeople. They're working hard to do their job, are overburdened and frazzled, and they don't need extra demands to do your business development.

The most common referral question is: "Do you know anybody who might need my service"? The typical response to this is, "No, not that I can think of, but I'll come back to you if somebody comes up". People respond like this because they don't know anybody called 'anybody', and in effect, you're asking them to do your research for you.

You, on the other hand, have already defined your target market and your model client. So be specific when describing the kind of person you want to be referred to. Suggest which company they might work for, their role and the type of challenges and ambitions they might have. The best method is to ask to be introduced to a specific individual—then it's easy for your client to agree or decline your request.

Anything that smooths the way for a client to refer you is worth doing, so why not hand them a referral pack consisting of your biography and company brochure? Identify ten people where there is mutual respect. I call this group the 'clique of 10. Then give them your referral pack, both hard copies and electronic, and tell them the type of person you want to talk to. Ask them to do the same so that you can give excellent quality referrals too.

The clique of 10 should be a mutually beneficial group where you give and receive referrals, helping and supporting each other in your businesses. Don't give a referral and expect one in return. It doesn't work like that. But if you provide referrals, over time, you'll receive referrals back, and the more you give, the more you get. Give referrals once a month and you'll often receive a reciprocal introduction.

So your recurring marketing activities in any one month are: to connect with your group of 80, network with your roll of 20, and refer to your clique of 10. Remember that these connections are all made on a person-to-person basis, where you reach out with something relevant and individualised. Create a regular daily/weekly/monthly cadence to establish a sustainable tempo. Mine is:

Connecting with my group of 80—four per day

Networking with my roll of 20—one per day

Generating referrals to and from my clique of 10—two or three per week

Do these one-to-one marketing activities in a disciplined way, and it will only take you around half an hour a day.

Step 7—Write A Book

You might not like the idea of writing, and if you don't want to write, then don't – this is Be Yourself Sales after all. But you could be missing a fantastic opportunity to establish yourself as an expert and raise your fees.

The primary purpose of writing a book is to share your knowledge with a broad audience. As an additional outcome, publishing a book will give you a sense of achievement, get you recognition, make an impression on the world and generate money.

The money you make from your book doesn't just come from book sales. The average number of copies an author sells by publishing through Amazon is 300. If your book sells for £9.99, you'll get around £1,500, which isn't much considering the amount of time, effort and passion you put into the process. But if you sold 300 books and gave another 300 away, that's 600 interested people who will have read your book and be more likely to work with you. In fact, most of your revenue from publishing comes from new assignments from people who have read your book.

The first thing you need to do is to get yourself a good writing coach. It doesn't matter how high or low you rate your abilities; a good coach will make your writing better. If you want people to read your book and hire you, it needs to present you in the best light. So, get a coach.

Next, define your target audience. You should have already settled on who is your model client and target market, so finding your audience should be straightforward. Before you put pen to paper, take a minute to decide if the book is for them, a wider audience, or even a narrower one, focusing on a specific subset of your target market.

When I started writing this book, I found the first few pages the hardest and it took me far too long to write the introduction. I would start, then decide it was the wrong direction or didn't touch on the points I wanted to discuss, and then delete it and start again. Goodness knows how many iterations I wrote before even starting on the first chapter.

That is, until I created a matrix or 'storyboard' of the overall book. Here is how it works:

Decide the title. Don't worry about getting it perfect as it will no doubt change before you get to the end of the process. However, deciding a title from the outset does help you get a clear picture in your head of what your book will be about.

Create a strapline. This is your foot-stomper, a short sentence under the title that provides further clarity on what the book is about and entices the reader to want to know more.

Draw a storyboard or matrix. I drew an empty table with 10–15 columns and 10–15 rows on a large piece of paper. The bigger the better, so use some A1 flipchart paper if you can.

Decide the main subjects you want to cover. Each column represents a chapter, so column one is chapter one etc. Write a chapter title for each subject above each column. Once completed, you'll have an outline of the book: a title, a strapline and the 10 or 15 chapters.

Populate the rows. The rows in your matrix represent the main points you want to cover in each chapter. Start with chapter one and work down the column. Write the main points you wish to include in that chapter, one point per row within the column. Repeat for the remaining sections and the main points for each chapter will be mapped out within the storyboard matrix.

You'll now have lots of ideas and themes to expand on to create your book.

Get writing. Write a few sentences per idea. This will come to around 300 words for each chapter, which is a good starting point.

Decide how long you want the book to be. Between 70,000 and 80,000 is the right size. If it's much longer, consider splitting it into two books. I'd rather sell two 70,000-word books at £8.99 than one with 140,000 words at £10.99. But be wary of making your book too long. Any longer than 80,000 words and most of your readers will not have the time or inclination to read it all.

Write the book quickly. There are so many half-written books out there, often because the budding author loses momentum. Staying the course comes down to discipline, focus and structure, so create some time in your schedule that occupies a recurring slot. It could be an hour a day, a day a week or a week a month, but whatever it is, establish a steady writing rhythm.

Let's say you dedicate two hours per day to writing your book. You write at a pace of one word in two seconds, which equates to thirty words per minute. Scale that up to two hours and you'll write 3,600 words a day. If you're disciplined and stick to the schedule, you'll have a book in around 20 days.

This example might sound logical, but in real life most people aren't that disciplined. Life gets in the way. Coaches and consultants are busy juggling clients and can't focus on writing to the exclusion of everything else.

So, we need to be realistic. Let's say a more feasible target is 5,000 words per week if you spend 50% or less of your time on fee-paying work. This would work out at 1,000 words per day, leaving two days of flex to cover the unforeseen. Even in this scenario you would be completing your first draft in three or four months. And if you're busier, reduce your target. If you're working with clients 100% of the time, aim for 500 words a day. If 75%, aim for 750.

Writing a book can be even quicker with the help of a little technology. Consider using a software package or mobile phone app that converts the spoken word into text. Writing a word takes an average of two seconds, but speaking it takes half a second. Scale that up and your draft manuscript could be ready in two months.

A good writing coach coupled with your own focus and discipline makes writing a good book faster and easier than you could imagine. Get the storyboard matrix right, and all the words will flow.

Step 8—Use Powerful Webinars

A webinar is an interactive online seminar that people register to join. Facebook and LinkedIn also offer 'live' broadcast sessions that are like webinars but without the need to register. I also consider these live broadcasts as webinars.

Broadcasting live events enables you to demonstrate your expertise and experience. It also allows you to showcase your services and give examples of the benefits you could help your audience achieve. One of the most significant advantages to webinars is convenience, as people can attend irrespective of their location. Think how easy it is compared to going to a seminar or conference where they'd need to travel and book a hotel room. For many people, committing time and money to an event like that is too much.

Webinars have the power to grab an audience's attention. They provide an ideal platform to have a two-way conversation and give attendees easy access to you. This is a great way to establish your presence. That's why large firms pay thousands of pounds to create slick, professional videos—studies show that up to 40% of webinar attendees become qualified leads.

When presenting your webinar it's essential to get your audience involved. You can either hold questions at the end so you can talk without being interrupted or invite people to post questions as you progress. I tend to mute all participants so it cuts out background noise but encourage them to raise questions at any time using the 'chat' function. This way, people can type questions live during the webinar and I can answer at the appropriate time.

The sooner you start answering questions the sooner you can demonstrate to your audience that they're not just watching a pre-recorded video. I have also found that answering questions early on encourages more questions to flow. This is the type of engagement you're looking for because it turns a one-way presentation into a two-way discussion.

As with any presentation or speech, a little planning can go a long way. Ask yourself these questions as part of your preparation:

Have I checked the software works and that I know how to use it?

Who will be attending and what are their challenges and ambitions?

What information will they want and what questions will they ask?

Does the presentation provide enough valuable information? While it's ok to mention your services, you need to make sure it doesn't sound like one long sales pitch.

Does the branding in the presentation match my website?

How will this look if someone joins the webinar using a mobile phone, and can they read the text? Expect half of the audience to be using their phone.

Have I prepared enough? Practise, refine and craft your presentation until it's perfect and you feel confident in its delivery.

Once your webinar is ready, go out and promote it. Make sure you let everyone in your group of 80, list of 20 and clique of 10 know it's taking place. Use social media to boost attendance and encourage people to explore your website.

Step 9—Manage Your Marketing

You'll need a customer relationship management (CRM) system to record and manage your marketing activity. There's a wide choice available, ranging from free software that provides basic functionality to expensive, complex, automated systems.

If you're a company managing hundreds of thousands of people, you'd need a comprehensive CRM system, but you only have 110 people to track, so a simple, low-cost software package will do just fine. Do some research and download and play with a few before deciding which one to choose—most systems offer free trials. Pick one that's cheap, easy to use and you like the look of.

You could create your own CRM system using a spreadsheet or database, but it's unlikely you have the in-depth knowledge and programming experience to create something effective. Considering that a functional CRM costs just £100–£200, it's not worth the effort. Better to save some time and buy one.

A CRM system holds all the data for your business contacts. This is your group of 80, your list of 20, and your clique of 10. Over time, the system will build up a history of your interactions with each person, your clients' past and preferences, assignments, emails, general notes and appointments.

Having all this data in one centralised platform gives a clear view of your sales cycle and the people flowing through it. This is invaluable to ensure each communication is unique and relevant to that individual. Each time you send a message or talk to someone, refer to the CRM to remind you where your conversation had got to and where to pick it up from.

This type of software can have many other functions: dashboards, alerts, integrations with other programmes—but you don't need them. Keep it simple.

Step 10—Check Your Readiness

The first three chapters of this book have identified the items you should have in place before attempting to sell your services. The next few will describe how to start having conversations with clients and win the work. This is a good point in the process to check you are ready before putting everything into action. Here's an overview of the work you should have done before progressing:

Building Brands

Building Brands taught us how to:

Pinpoint the type of people you want as clients and research them to understand their challenges and ambitions. Then align your services to address their needs and wishes.

Be clear on your target market and who your model clients are.

Determine their challenges and ambitions.

Articulate how your service satisfies their requirements.

Practise talking about what you do until you feel confident and comfortable.

In short, you should know the group of people you serve, what they want and need, how you satisfy their requirements and be able to talk about it confidently and naturally.

Constructing Credibility

Constructing Credibility showed us how to:

Get all the assumed and basic credibility builders in place first. Then put into practice the things that will delight potential new clients to enhance credibility and trust.

Have all the basics in place: a good LinkedIn profile, a website, an email address, professional photographs, a high-quality company brochure, one-page service overviews and client testimonials.

Set your standards of service.

Produce a series of interesting and informative articles.

Develop assets or processes that will delight clients.

In short, you should have everything in place that will establish you as a trustworthy expert, dedicated to serving a specific set of people.

Positioning Pricing

Positioning Pricing taught us to:

Calculate the financial value you generate for clients.

Then outline the return on the client's investment to make it easy for them to say "yes."

Monetise the benefits you help clients achieve.

Calculate the client's ROI.

Set your payment structure.

Decide if you're going to offer any discounts.

In short, you should be able to justify your fees with confidence and be comfortable with the terms of payment.

Managing Marketing

Managing Marketing taught us how to:

Build deeper relations with existing contacts, expand your network and get introduced to more people who are relevant to your business.

Create your group of 80, list of 20, and clique of 10.

Meet people at networking events and on LinkedIn.

Have broadcasting software in place and be ready to promote and run webinars.

Hire a writing coach and start to write daily or weekly.

In short, you should have started to promote your services in a way that is genuine and authentic and not considered pushy or intrusive.

❋ ❋ ❋

Ten Steps To Manage Marketing

Step 1—Focus your marketing
Step 2—Create marketing materials
Step 3—Connect with friends

Step 4—Meet new people
Step 5—Network on LinkedIn
Step 6—Ask for referrals
Step 7—Write a book
Step 8—Use powerful webinars
Step 9—Manage your marketing
Step 10—Check your readiness

COMMENCING CONVERSATIONS

What

Meeting a potential client for the first few times will make or break your future relationship with them. Start by having a conversation that shows you're interested in finding out more about them.

Why

At this point in the sales cycle, it's unlikely you'll have built enough trust for a client to ask for your help. If you lapse into 'sales mode' too early, you'll push them away.

How

Establish an authentic rapport, then move on to understand what support they need. Determine if you can help and find out if they want your assistance.

※ ※ ※

Gillian Sandstrom PhD, a senior lecturer in psychology at the University of Essex, conducted a study on how people feel when they have a conversation with someone they don't know.

She found that, before the conversation, most people expected to find their conversation partner interesting. After the conversation, most people reported that this was in fact the case. However, when asked whether they thought their conversation partner would find *them* interesting, the majority of the same people didn't think they would. Sandstrom said, "Nearly everyone reported that the conversation went way better than they thought. [This shows that,] if conversations feel awkward, they're probably going better than you think."

Talking to new people can be difficult because there are lots of unknowns. Sandstrom agrees. She says, "We go into conversations thinking all these awful things can happen."

Think back to the last great conversation you had. What did you do and say? Were you warm, funny, thoughtful or logical? What did the other person say and do? Are there standard practices you can use to help you have an enjoyable, authentic and productive discussion? The answer is "yes".

In *How to Win Friends and Influence People,* Dale Carnegie says that, when it comes to professional services, people buy relationships first, benefits second, price third and technical approaches last.

When you have a conversation with a potential client, focus on the relationship first. Try not to be too focused on the technical stuff, but make every effort to help the client feel comfortable and like you on a personal level. The steps in this chapter are based on Dale Carnegie's book, which shows it is still as relevant today as it was when it was first published in 1937.

Step 1—Ditch The Pitch

The purpose of an initial discussion with a client is not to pitch your services. You won't sell an assignment on the first meeting unless the client has an urgent problem that needs fixing straight away. So, make the first meeting all about them. Treat it as a fact-finding and relationship-building mission.

Unconfident people rely on a pre-written pitch; confident people talk with authenticity from the heart. Who wants to listen to a pre-planned, pre-packaged monologue that's trying to sell something? Not me. In the 1940s and 50s the thirty-second pitch was a popular way of selling, but like many ideas from that era, it has not aged well. So why do people still use a pitch? It sounds trite, stale and tired. Above all, it sounds like a script: over the top and all about you. It feels like you're forcing yourself on your client, and it smacks of someone who isn't confident in their services.

There are a few theories about where the pitch approach came from, but the most widely accepted version is that it originated from the studio days in Hollywood.

The story goes that the aspiring author or screenwriter trying to capture the attention of a film executive would only get five minutes to pitch their idea. If they were lucky, they would get another ten minutes to explain it further until someone eventually said "yes".

This approach was adopted by businesses in the early 2000s when there was a rapid growth of technology start-ups looking for funding. Young hopefuls would stalk investors and blurt out their elevator pitch in the hope of getting their attention and some more time to explain.

If you're tempted to use this approach, throw that thought in the bin. Imagine yourself chasing a potential client, grabbing their arm and holding on to it so you can blurt out how great you are. The only thing the client will be thinking is about how to get away from you.

You're not a screenwriter selling a script or a whizz kid selling a new app. You're a service professional aiming to build long and trusting relationships.

So, what's the best way to do that? Be yourself. Relax and have an authentic conversation by listening to what they say.

Step 2—Establish Warm Rapport

A genuine rapport helps to establish likeability, and it's the best way to develop an authentic personal connection. Some people are naturally gifted in creating rapport; others have to work at it. Either way, if you want to win new clients and raise your fees, you need to make your potential client like you.

First and foremost, don't try to be someone you are not and don't act like you think someone else would expect. That includes adopting a smooth or bombastic sales tone. Relax, smile and go in with an optimistic mindset. Good things will follow. As Oscar Wilde said, "Be yourself; everyone else is already taken."

A smile will radiate friendliness and sincerity. People are drawn to happy people and avoid those who look grumpy and unapproachable. Smiling is free and it generates a lot of goodwill. It enriches those who receive it without taking away from the person giving it. In fact, the giver also gains.

Frosty people get chilly reactions from other people, so approach rapport building with the intention of being warm and welcoming. Smile, give a firm handshake and make eye contact. Actions speak louder than words and a smile says, "I like you" and "I am open to talk with you". It's the perfect way to use body language as a precursor to a pleasant conversation.

Make every effort to take a genuine interest in clients. Some people parade through life self-obsessed, interested only in promoting themselves and getting people involved in them. This behaviour seldom works.

People are not all that interested in you—it's not in their nature. They're too concerned with their own challenges and ambitions to consider yours, so your conversations shouldn't be about you, they should be about them. People can be self-obsessed—it's not a criticism, just a fact of life. Learn about your client before and during a sales meeting before proposing a solution to their problem. Show interest in them as individuals as well as in their challenges.

People like to hear their name used by others because it

shows that they've paid attention. If you say someone's name when you're having a conversation you're effectively paying them a compliment. Make an effort to remember people's names by focusing and fixing them in your memory. Practise recollecting someone's name by repeating it in your head until you can remember them.

Remembering and saying a client's name will create value and goodwill and make them feel important. Philosophers have speculated for thousands of years about human relationships. The most famous of them—Buddha, Confucius, Lao-tse and Jesus to mention a few—summed it up in one thought: "Treat others as you would like them to treat you." It's a good rule for both your professional and personal life. Talk to people about themselves and they will listen. These principles are undying and shared by all humans.

Some sales books encourage people to make small talk to build rapport. For example, you might be told to look around the potential client's office and talk about what you see. "Ah, I see you have a bike tucked away in the corner. Do you cycle into work every day? I can't imagine battling the city traffic in the morning. How do you find it?"

But rapport building is not based on giving planned, fake compliments. The mentality behind it is dishonest and disingenuous. Your client will know what you're doing, and it could damage your new relationship if it's done clumsily.

Or you might be tempted at a sales meeting to fill all the scheduled time with business talk. But approaching an important meeting with the assumption that you'll need the full hour to get your key messages across is also flawed. It's worth having some informal discussion before launching straight into the business at hand, because clients want to know if you're the type of person they'll enjoy working with. If you jump right in at the beginning of a meeting with "Ok, let me tell you about my great services", you'll create a tense atmosphere. Give the client a chance to take a breath and say "hello".

You'll be able to judge what is the right amount of rapport

to build in each situation before starting to talk business. Too little and you'll create an atmosphere of formal abruptness; the conversation will take on a staccato, clipped air. But too much time chatting and the buyer will wonder, "Are we ever going to get moving?" Get the balance right and be authentic.

Step 3—Dance With Them

We all know what it feels like when we've established authentic rapport. When two people 'click', that sense of linkage feels enjoyable and natural. Daniel Goleman's book *Social Intelligence* explores this phenomenon and identifies two key ingredients: 'attention' and 'coordination'.

Two-way attention facilitates a sense of shared feelings, but it's more than making the client feel comfortable. Social comfort can be established through fake rapport building. This is when the client feels relaxed, but they don't have the sense of you tuning in to their feelings.

The matching of tone of voice and facial expressions signals attentiveness, and your non-verbal messages matter more than what you're saying.

Think of a parent having to tell their child the lousy news a pet dog has died. The parent can deliver terrible news while still displaying warmth and care through their voice and body language. The child is being told the worst news they could imagine, but they still feel positivity and love.

Have you ever noticed when you walk with someone that within minutes you've synchronised your steps? The same thing happens when people talk in rapport. You can see non-verbal coordination and mirroring, and the two people bounce off each other like dance partners.

We coordinate through subtle non-verbal methods such as the timing of physical movements and the pace of our words. At these moments, both you and the client feel enlivened and able to express your thoughts. If two people lack coordination, they feel awkward, with misjudged responses and uneasy pauses.

Daniel Goleman says that the more two people synchronise their movements and mannerisms during a conversation, the more positive they will feel about each other. He continues to say:

> *Whenever two people are in rapport, we can see an 'emotional dance'; flashing eyebrows, rapid hand gestures, fleeting facial expressions, swiftly adjusted word pacing, shifts of gaze. Such coordination lets us connect and, if we do so well, feel a positive emotional resonance with the other person.*

The more we dance, the stronger the relationship. When it comes to professional services, people buy people, so if you find a potential model client, don't be afraid to open up and go for a waltz.

Step 4—Project Steadfast Confidence

From the professional consultant or perceptive coach to the captivating speaker, everyone needs confidence. Clients will look for it in you, because it shows that you know what you're doing and have done it many times before. If someone's going to buy your services, they don't want to be the guinea pig.

Confidence is vital for most aspects of work and life, yet service professionals often fail to hide their nervousness. This creates a negative cycle for consultants and coaches, as their lack of confidence reduces their ability to get work.

Potential clients won't want to hire you if you fumble your way through a meeting and blurt out a panicky, rambling monologue. Nervousness translates to physical signals which make you look uncomfortable. In turn this makes the person you are meeting uneasy, too.

Project steadfast confidence by speaking clearly, looking the person in the eye and adopting a relaxed body language. Listen to the client and admit when you don't know the answer to all their questions.

Confident people put others at ease and inspire belief. This creates a positive cycle where gaining the faith of others enables them to go on and become successful, further reinforcing their own confidence.

But how do you build a sense of balanced self-confidence? Is it something you can fake? The good news is that you won't have to—it's possible to become more confident if you're willing to do the work.

Confidence is born from achieving the goals you set and the challenges laid down by others. I bet if you sit down for ten minutes and reflect on all the things you've achieved this year there will be a lot to be proud of. Perhaps you reached the highest sales figures in your team three months in a row, or you helped a client achieve something no one else was able to do.

Whatever your achievements, note them down in a long list so you can refer to them. At the start of each day, open the notebook and take a minute to acknowledge that you've done some great things. Confirm to yourself the skills, experience and determination that you needed to achieve these successes. You are great at what you do, your clients know it, and it's about time you knew it too.

Step 5—Listen To Them

You'll know by now that I'm against the 'elevator pitch' style of selling. It's used by insecure salespeople trying to get their message across to people who are not interested.

Instead, it's important to recognise that a client conversation is not an opportunity for you to impress them; it's a chance for you to listen. Concentrate on what's being said and not being said rather than hearing the basics of their message and jumping to interject.

You must also be *seen* to be listening. Otherwise, the client will have the impression that you're not interested even if you are. Use verbal and non-verbal indicators to convey interest in what's being said. Maintain eye contact (but don't stare), nod and smile, or make affirmative sounds that encourage them to continue with the discussion. Ask open questions, don't fill silences with comments or questions and let the conversation 'breathe'. Remember that some silence is good, as it helps both you and the client to gather your thoughts and avoid rambling on.

Remember that most people you talk to will be more interested in what they have to say than in listening to you. They're more concerned about their challenges and ambitions than yours, so stop talking so much and listen to what they say.

Step 6—Uncover Their Needs

At some point in your conversation, the talk will move from general rapport building to the client's professional situation. You need to uncover what the client needs. In most cases, the client will raise the topic, but if they don't, you should nudge them in that direction.

If you don't understand their current challenges and future ambitions, how can you have a sales conversation? How will you know if you can help them? You won't. These are the things you should find out early on in the discussion.

Some open and friendly questions that show your interest in them should move the conversation towards business. "What are you working on?" invites them to talk about what's on their mind without being too direct. "How's business?" enables them to open up about their current challenges. You're an expert in your field, so you'll know what's going on in their sector. You could ask, "I'm told supply chain costs are rising in your sector. Are you in the same position?" It's a little more direct but not pointed enough to make the client feel uncomfortable.

Try using these questions or, better still, find your own words. The important thing is to steer the conversation towards finding out their needs.

Once you know the challenges they're facing you can dig a little deeper. "How is that affecting you?" "Is it affecting other people, too?" "What are you looking to achieve?" "When are you aiming to start and complete the work?"

Once you've uncovered the person's needs, it's time to move on to visualising what success would look like for them. Visualisation creates emotion, which is critical to selling services. Ask questions that can help both you and the client gain a deeper understanding of their motivations: "How would you know when you've achieved it?" What are the outcomes? "What will be the tangible and intangible results?" "How will you feel?"

Here are some other questions you could ask:

Could you tell me a bit about your work and your role?

Did anything trigger you asking for this conversation?

How were things going before that trigger occurred?

What exactly do you want?

Why is that important to you?

What do you want instead of the current situation?

What needs to change?

What would happen if you did nothing to change it?

What do you want to see, hear and feel when you achieve it?

If you attain your goal, what will it mean to you?

How long do you want it to take?

When do you want to achieve your ambition?

If I understand what you're saying correctly, you are.... Is that right?

What have you tried to do so far to resolve the issue?

What is your feeling about needing to change?

Replay these emotions back to them to confirm you understand not only the logical reasoning but also the emotional factors. Now draw out the positive experience the client would enjoy if they addressed their pressing challenge or achieved that ambition. What would be their emotions if their dreams come true? Help them taste the pride, success, happiness, wealth, confidence and more.

Step 7—Establish An Interest

Some people aren't comfortable with the next part of the conversation, but it's crucial. It can't be avoided as it's the first stepping stone to asking for the business. It's to ask the client to indicate if they're open to receiving help.

When you ask this question, it's essential to do it in an acceptable way that's not too direct. Otherwise you'll bring the conversation to a shuddering end. Of course, the potential client might tell you that they're looking for support without prompting, but most of the time you'll need to ask.

Even when the conversation is moving in a promising direction, it doesn't necessarily mean they want help. Don't get excited and assume the client is going to offer a juicy assignment—they might not want you. They might be looking for one of your contacts. I've had informal chats with lots of people I thought could be a potential client, only for them to turn around and ask *me* for work.

Here are some questions that can bring the conversation around to the client acknowledging that they need some support:

What are your beliefs about coaching/consulting?

What would coaching/consulting need to do to address your challenges?

Have you had a coach/consultant before? How did that work out?

Are you considering using a coach/consultant?

Is there anything stopping you from hiring a coach/consultant?

What was it that made you consider using me?

What are you looking for in a coach/consultant?

If it feels like they're looking for help but just haven't said it, then ask them. Say, "Are you looking for support?" "Are you thinking about using some external help?" "Do you have the motivation to work with a coach/consultant to achieve this?"

Again, you can use these examples or find your own words, whatever suits you best.

Step 8—State Your Interest

If your potential client gives a positive response indicating that they're seeking help, it's important to tell them that you'd like to work with them—provided they fit your model client profile, of course.

State your interest clearly: "I would like to work with you on this" or "I believe I can help". Or perhaps "This area is my speciality and I'd be happy to provide support." Nothing fancy, no longwinded monologues, just let them know you'd like to work with them.

After telling them your interest, reinforce how well matched you are for each other. This is where having a personal connection is critical when providing a professional service. There's nothing wrong with telling them that they're your model client. In fact, I encourage you to do so. "I'd love to work with you because you are my model client" or "I think we'd do some great work together as you'd be my perfect client". Or perhaps "You fit my ideal client profile." As with the other questions and phrases, be yourself and say it in a way that reflects your personality.

When you say this, the person you're talking to might look a little confused. Or they might be direct and tell you they don't understand your comment. Perhaps not many people have called them 'ideal' or 'perfect' before. It might catch them off guard.

This is your opportunity to tell them why you think the assignment would work out well. For example, "I noticed you're creative, open to feedback and unafraid to speak your mind." Then you continue: "I tend to do my best work with people with the same positive work ethics as you".

When was the last time somebody recognised your good qualities like that? It might have been a long time since someone gave them a compliment. At the very least they'll appreciate it and it will create a stronger bond. You'll show them that you don't just work with anybody—you choose your clients, and you've chosen them. They'll also see that you're someone who understands them and does their best work with people just like them.

Of course, you might decide that the person you're talking to isn't right for you. They might not be your model client. It can be tempting to take them on as a client anyway—you'd be turning down money after all. But don't fill your work schedule with less than ideal clients. You'll grow to dislike the work and perform under par. The best thing to do is to tell them you're too busy to take on a new client or say you think they'd be better served by someone else. If you can, refer them to one of your clique of 10.

Step 9—Confirm Shared Interest

So your potential client has said they'd like to work with you, and you've confirmed that you'd like to work with them. It's now time to tell them *how* you can help and *how much* it will cost.

At this stage in your relationship keep your description at a high level. Keep it light; don't go into detail. Tell the client how you would approach the assignment and the methodologies that might be appropriate. But don't commit to a specific solution—you should take some time to think through the intricacies of the assignment and write your chosen methodology in your proposal.

Once the potential client seems comfortable with your approach, you need to test the price. There's no point writing a proposal if the person is not able or willing to pay for your services. While you should avoid giving a specific quote as you'll need to double-check details before coming up with a final figure, you can test their appetite by providing a price bracket. You might float a price by saying "high five figures" or "low four figures", for example, or any other bracket that gives a rough indication.

The potential client will have one of two responses: they'll either nod and say that's around what they were thinking or they'll raise their eyebrows and tell you it's far too much. In the latter case, you have two avenues to choose from. The first is to stick to your guns and say, "Well, that's roughly how much it will cost, but your potential return on investment far outweighs it." Remember: your fees are based on the value you generate.

Or, you can ask how much they were thinking to pay, and then scale down your proposed solution to suit. Both you and the buyer need to be in the same ballpark when it comes to fees before you write a proposal however, or it will be a waste of everyone's time.

A word to the wise. The level of support you offer and the value of your proposal should correspond to how much trust you've established. If this is the first time you've had a sales conversation with this client and you haven't worked with them before, their confidence in you will not be established. In this case you should start by offering something small—a low barrier to entry solution that doesn't cost much. This approach helps negate the perceived risk, as not many people will spend hundreds of thousands on you if they haven't worked with you before. So, start small, provide an excellent service, build up their confidence in you, and then you can begin to offer more complete solutions at a higher price. Start small, build confidence, end big.

When the conversation is nearing its end, try to summarise what's been agreed. There are two main reasons to do this. Firstly, it allows you to check that you've understood what the client has said, and secondly, it provides an opportunity for you to check if your proposed solution is on the right path.

If they answer "yes" to both your summarisation and your outline solution, then the probability of them becoming your newest client increases.

Step 10—Agree Next Steps

Avoid letting the conversation drift and fizzle out as your coffee goes cold and you ask for the bill. It's vital that you don't leave that conversation until you've agreed what will happen next and set a date for a follow-up meeting. If you say, "So where do we go from here?", you'll lose control of the conversation, as 90% of the time their answer will be "Let me think about it and

I'll come back to you." Then they'll walk out of that coffee shop never to be seen again.

Your aim is to get a proposal to them tomorrow, or by the following day at the latest. Close the discussion by telling them that's what you're going to do, but phrase it as a question: "If it's ok with you, I'll send over a proposal tomorrow for your review. Is that ok?" They always say "yes." Then ask if anyone else should receive a copy, if there Is someone else involved in the decision. They always say "no."

Now tell them that you'd like to meet them the day after you send the proposal to talk through the contents and answer any questions they might have. Time is the enemy of making a sale, so make sure you're meeting as soon as possible. The longer you leave it, the more time the client will have to come up with a reason not to proceed. Strike while the iron's hot.

Your conversations should be relaxed, friendly and focused on the client. Don't try to sell your services at the first meeting unless they have an urgent, pressing problem. During the follow-up meetings, they'll start to open up about their challenges and concerns. This is the right time to move the conversation to discuss how you could help.

❉ ❉ ❉

Ten Steps To Commence Conversations

Step 1—Ditch the pitch
Step 2—Establish warm rapport
Step 3—Dance with them
Step 4—Project steadfast confidence
Step 5—Listen to them
Step 6—Uncover their needs
Step 7—Establish their interest
Step 8—State your interest

Step 9—Confirm shared interest
Step 10—Agree next steps

PREPARING PROPOSALS

What

Write a concise, persuasive proposal that is easy to read and understand. The document should be set in a logical flow and serve as a legal contract once signed.

Why

The quicker you submit the proposal, the higher the chance of the client saying "yes." Proposals always work best when they are short and in a standard format. They should be quick to write and easy for the client to understand.

How

Show you understand their situation, convince them you can help and demonstrate that the benefits outweigh the costs.

❋ ❋ ❋

I'm a big fan of having a standard structure for proposals. It ensures you include all the essential points and that you express them in a logical and easy to understand format. More importantly, it helps to speed up the process of writing the proposal and submitting it to your future client.

When you have a conversation with a potential client, there will come the point where they will either ask for, or you will offer to send, a proposal. Having a standard structure allows you to say with confidence, "I'll get it over to you tomorrow".

This will do two things. It will show them that you're enthusiastic about working with them, and it will indicate that you're professional and responsive. The proposal will then land in their inbox when it is still fresh in their mind. This accelerated delivery of the proposal will allow you to have a follow-up meeting to win the work in short order.

Unless your proposal is going to be distributed amongst a group of stakeholders, the document should be confirmatory. That is, most of the information has already been discussed and agreed during your conversations. The proposal is to add detail and formalise the agreement to proceed with the assignment. It's an explanation, not a justification, and it's not a persuasion tool for you to make a sale. Nor is it to be used for you and the buyer to start a negotiation. A proposal should be submitted once the approach, and the price bracket, has been agreed.

For this reason I don't have an 'introduction' section within a standard proposal unless I know there are other people involved. If there are, it's worth having one so that everyone understands how and why the initial conversation started. But most of the time the conversations will have been with the decision-maker. The proposal is going to the client, and they already know the circumstances that initiated it.

For a proposal to serve as a formal contract, it should contain three things: a clear explanation of each person's responsibilities, the terms and conditions, and a section for the client to sign. Don't add anything that hasn't been discussed with your client or it will raise doubts and questions. You've worked hard to establish your credibility; don't blow it at the final stage.

The length of the document is determined by the value and complexity of the assignment, so you'll need to provide more information on the approach and methodology if it's a com-

, intricate project. In general, the more the assignment the more detailed you'll need to make the proposal. Here a general guide:

Less than £10,000—two to four pages

£10,000–£100,000—five to ten pages

£100,000–£250,000—ten to twelve pages

More than £250,000—fifteen pages maximum, with additional information in the appendices

Nine main sections make up my 'go-to' proposal structure, and I would suggest you adopt something similar. They are:

1. Challenges and concerns

2. Objectives and ambitions

3. Metrics and targets

4. Benefits and outcomes

5. Approach and methodology

6. Solutions and options

7. Timing and resources

8. Acceptance and authorisation

9. Accountabilities and terms

The first four sections set the scene and should have been discussed with the client beforehand—nothing in these sections should come as a surprise to the reader. They are to align and confirm each party has the same understanding of what needs to be improved.

Sections five through nine are to define how you are going to address their challenges and for the client to agree to the work. They are for you to present the solutions and to gain the authority to proceed.

Step 1—Demonstrate You Understand

The challenges and concerns section is where you summarise your client's current situation. The 'challenge' is the problem or group of problems they're facing, and the 'concern' is the negative consequences that will occur if the challenges are not dealt with.

First, write a few paragraphs about your client's challenges, and then proceed to highlight the concerns. You're aiming to have the reader nodding their head in recognition. This will give them more confidence and believe you understand their predicament, so show that you 'get it' and 'get them'. Demonstrate that you've worked with other people in a similar situation to resolve their problems and warn them of the potential risks if they do nothing.

It's vital to convey your client's challenges and concerns dispassionately. You don't want to be perceived as mocking them by being overly sympathetic, but it's essential to make clear the seriousness of the situation. Think of it as a doctor telling a patient the results of a medical diagnosis. Be respectful, but lay out the prognosis.

You can gauge the client's personality and characteristics to inform the language you use. For example, if they're forceful and to the point then you can be a little more direct—they'll respect you for it. If they're more emotional or perhaps even spiritual, your prognosis should be more reflective and balanced. Highlight both the positive and negative observations, but don't shy away from the truth.

Matching your written style with your client's personality will help your proposal to resonate with the reader. The structure of your proposal should be standard, but the content will always be unique.

It's important to make clear whether the information about their current situation has come from your discussion or from your own direct observation. When writing this section, you'll need to include caveats if the description of the challenges and concerns have not come from you. You can do this at the start by using simple phrases like "I have been told that…." or you can do it at the end by stating something like "The opinions and descriptions given in this section will need to be validated at the start of the assignment."

My preference is the former. State at the beginning of the proposal that the information has been given by someone else through conversation. It will then be implicit that you'll need to confirm what you've been told once the work starts. For example, you might be a productivity improvement consultant and the client has told you their call centre staff are well trained. You'll need to take them at their word at this stage but will want to confirm once the assignment has started.

Or you might be a life coach and the client has told you they perform 20 minutes of Tai Chi every morning. Again, you should believe what you've been told and confirm it after the coaching begins.

Everything you write in this section of your proposal should come from what you have been told, given or observed. Remember: you want the reader to be nodding in agreement. Don't introduce any new observations or thoughts that haven't already been discussed, as you don't want to raise any questions that require supplementary information or an updated proposal later. This will slow down the authorisation of the assignment, and the longer it takes to get your proposal signed off, the less chance you have of winning the work.

Step 2—State the objectives

The objectives and ambitions section is where you record the things the client hopes to achieve. The objectives are the specified outcomes—the result you and the client are working towards. You must accomplish these if the assignment is to be judged a success. The ambitions are the things the client hopes to achieve over and above the objectives. The client will be happy if you meet the objectives, and they'll be delighted if they attain their ambitions.

You'll need to achieve the customer's objectives before thinking about working on their ambitions. These are the icing on the cake, but no matter how fancy the icing is, your client won't be happy if there's no cake.

Objectives = cake
Ambitions = icing

I prefer to focus on just one primary objective, but in any case try to have no more than three. Articulate them in a clear, concise manner so there are no doubts about what the work aims to achieve. My objective is to get the person I'm working with more clients. Clear, simple and easy to understand.

If you've been given five or ten objectives, the scope of the assignment is too broad. The client is expecting too much. It might be the case that there *are* a lot of objectives and the client insists they must be achieved. In this case, suggest structuring the assignment as a programme consisting of three to five discrete projects. Then propose to the client the sequencing and timing of the projects. Keep yourself and your client focused by working on one project at a time. Price each project and offer a bundle price with a discount if the client commits to them all in advance.

In most circumstances, neither you nor your client will have performed a great deal of analysis together before starting the work. So it will be near impossible to quantify the benefits with any level of confidence.

Describe the objectives but without putting a value on them. For example:

To reduce the cost of production

To increase staff retention

To re-energise and motivate the board of directors

To teach the middle management team how to coach others

To regain control of a project

To improve customer satisfaction

To streamline the supply chain

Set them out so they are obvious and unmistakable.

The 'ambitions' are the elements that, if achieved, will be considered as extraordinary results. When you help a client attain these, they'll be transformed from a client into an advocate. Advocates will promote your services and become a rich source of referrals.

Aim to have double the number of ambitions as objectives. If you have two objectives, there should be four ambitions. So, if your aim is to reduce the cost of your client's manufacturing costs, two ambitions might be:

To reduce the lead time of production

To reduce the level of inventory within the production facility

In this example, you must reduce the cost—that is a given. If you can also reduce the lead-time or inventory, your client will be singing your praises for years.

Another example might be if you're a coach with an assignment to re-energise and motivate a board of directors. In this case, the client has set out two primary objectives:

To help the board become more positive and forward-looking during board meetings

To help the board re-engage with the company's vision and mission and promote these to the workforce.

The ambitions flow from the objectives. Although not essential to the assignment's success, they are things that would be nice to achieve. In this example the board might agree to these ambitions:

To reduce the level of conflict between board members and to pro-actively support each other

To reduce the length of the board meetings, specifically to reduce the time consumed by debates

To become living, breathing examples of the company's vision and mission

To cascade these to the workforce and enthuse them with a renewed sense of purpose and energy

Always prioritise the objectives over the ambitions. The client is paying you to achieve the objectives. The ambitions are the 'cherry on top', so make sure the client understands these are not the primary mission.

Step 3—Set The Targets

All metrics are not created equal. Useful metrics need targets to provide a context in which to judge success and the measures you choose should align with your client's objectives and ambitions. Use two types of metrics for each objective and ambition:

Leading indicators. These measure the things that need to be done to achieve the targets. They are the inputs to effect the desired change.

Lagging indicators. These measure the outcomes and tell you if the goal has been obtained. They are the outputs of the work.

For demonstration purposes let's use the previous example where the objective is to reduce the manufacturing company's cost of production. Defining the lagging indicator is straightforward: it's the cost per unit. The leading indicators measure what needs to be done to achieve that outcome. These will include the main factors that are causing the additional costs you're going to address. These might consist of the defect rate of the manufacturing process and how much time is lost to the machines breaking down.

Don't be weighed down by analysis paralysis by using too many metrics. Pick one lagging indicator and two or three leading indicators.

Metrics are most effective when they have a target and a date for when that is to be achieved. However, as I've already said, you shouldn't commit to a specific target before the assignment starts. You want a robust and long-lasting relationship with the client, so honesty is the best policy. You don't know what levels of performance can be achieved before the assignment starts. The proposal is a legal document—would you want to commit to something based on a guess?

Your client will want and expect the proposal to describe how much their situation will improve, but you're not able to state a specific value. There is a two-stage process to deal with this. The proposal should set out a range of potential performances, then explain that the particular target will be agreed after the first phase of your work is completed. That way, you'll provide the client with an indication of what's feasible and you'll have enough data to make an accurate judgement soon after.

So how do you word all of this in your proposal? Going back to the example of the factory that wants to reduce costs, a leading indicator is the downtime of the production machine. Your proposal would state:

"A leading indicator is to reduce the amount of time machine XYZ is not running. The downtime will be measured by the number of minutes lost each day. I have not observed the machine or analysed the data to determine the target level performance. However, you should expect a reduction of between 25% to 50%."

This allows the client to understand the potential benefit of hiring you but does not tie you down to a specific target. It's better to be honest with the client rather than be too confident before you know the facts.

Step 4—Quantify Financial Benefits

Your proposal should make financial sense to your client by showing that they'll get more out than they put in. Therefore, it's important that you monetise each metric and the accompanying range of potential benefits.

I tend to include a table to say what the metrics are, the range of potential improvements and how that equates to the financial benefit. Here's an example:

Quality Improvement	4%	6%	8%	10%	12%
Financial benefit	£1,000	£6,000	£11,000	£16,000	£21,000

It demonstrates that I am expecting to improve the quality of the client's process by between 4% and 12%, providing a financial benefit ranging from £1,000 to £21,000. Make sure the lowest monetary value is a least twice the client's investment.

Any lower and it's not worth the client's effort.

The person buying your services must feel confident they will get more money back than their investment. Some coaches might not find it so easy to calculate the financial return they generate (the ROI or Return on Investment). Their main benefits might be based on improving confidence, energy and resilience. But even in these cases, an ROI can be calculated with some careful thought.

Even if the ROI isn't at the forefront of the client's mind, it will help their justification. For some clients, having a substantial ROI is the 'cake' and for others it's the 'icing'. Either way, it's essential to calculate and present it in your proposal.

To calculate the ROI, the financial benefit is divided by the financial cost. For example, if a client was to buy a service for £1,000 and as a result gain £2,000 of benefit, the ROI would be two. Remember that the financial benefit is generated either by more money coming in or less money going out. A strong ROI provides an overwhelming justification for the client to purchase your services.

There are two types of financial benefit: 'recurring' and 'non-recurring'. Let's say you reduce a client's financial outgoings every month or year; you would define this as a recurring benefit. If the monthly cost reduction came to £2,000 per month, it would equate to a £24,000 annual saving. I state financial benefits over three years, so in this example, the economic benefit equates to £72,000.

Imagine if your fee structure was based on the time for money model and you were charging a client £1,000. You'd soon realise that you're not charging enough. How much would you raise your fees if you knew your client was getting an ROI of 72?

Don't be tempted to use a longer duration than three years to artificially boost the ROI. People can envisage three years into the future, but if you talk about a five- or ten-year period it becomes more of an academic exercise. Three years is just right, as it leverages the value of the recurring benefits but within a tangible time frame.

Non-recurring financial benefits are when you help a client make an improvement that generates a one-off financial benefit. This might be, for example, if you help a client sell a house for more money. You might charge a client £5,000 to work your magic and sell the house for £25,000 above its current market value, generating a return of five times the client's investment. This benefit isn't recurring; once the house is sold, the client cannot continue to sell the same house multiple times.

For non-recurring benefits, the client needs to believe that investing their money in your services will generate more money than their initial outlay.

Here's an example of a proposal that quantifies the ROI through a combination of recurring and non-recurring benefits:

Client outlay for your service = £4,000

Recurring benefit #1 = £1,000/year
Recurring benefit #2 = £3,000/year
Recurring benefit #3 = £1,000/year

Total recurring benefits = £5,000/year
Total recurring benefits over 3 years = £15,000

Non-recurring benefit #4 = £5,000

Total benefits over 3 years = £20,000

ROI £4,000/£20,000 = 5

Your client will get five times more than they paid over three years.

As we discussed in chapter three, Positioning Pricing, too many people only consider direct financial outcomes. They are missing other factors that could generate a more significant financial result. That's why using the 'five Es' format is useful for identifying additional sources of financial benefit.

The 'economy' element is the obvious direct financial benefits that come from the objectives defined for the assignment.

Use the four remaining 'Es' as a framework to identify other ways of boosting the ROI.

Effectiveness: What tasks, processes or people will become more productive or effective? Quantify how much these things cost. Establish if the changes will reduce these costs or even increase income. You might be surprised how much additional financial benefit it could create.

Efficiency: What elements of the client's business will move quicker, be more reliable and operate more smoothly? Perhaps through your excellent work a process will run faster and, as a result, inventories will reduce. This decrease could free up more cash, consume less space to hold the stock and minimise costs from heating, lighting, IT systems and people.

Emotional and Environmental: These categories might not present obvious sources of financial benefit, but on closer inspection they can also provide opportunities. How many of your clients (or their employees) are not at work due to mental or physical health conditions? What if the changes you implement help to reduce absenteeism by 50%? If our fictitious client's organisation has, on average, ten people absent throughout the year and their average salary is £70,000, the financial benefits of five people returning to work would be £350,000.

Your work might improve staff engagement. It's hard to quantify improved engagement, but it's always worth searching for indicators. There might be a defunct employee suggestion scheme that previously generated £500,000 of savings a year. Perhaps the client implemented a new working practice six months ago, after which the suggestions dried up. You might apply a solution to resolve the disputed working practice that members are happy to adopt and, as a result, the flow of ideas improves. If you can prove a correlation and causation, the client will accept the cause and effect.

You can tap into a rich stream of indirect financial benefits if you think about it carefully. Quite often, the value of indirect benefits outweighs the more obvious direct sources.

In summary, your proposal must make financial sense. Don't commit to a specific target or monetary value, but provide a range. Calculate recurring and non-recurring benefits and set these out over three years. Look for financial gains from direct sources, and search further and broader to identify the full range of economic benefits.

Step 5—Describe The Methodology

A client buys the benefits and outcomes of your work, not the tools and techniques you've spent years perfecting. It's easy for coaches and consultants to become too proud of their approach and forget that a client buys results first and methodology second.

Your client isn't buying 'value stream mapping', 'brainstorming' or 'tabletop emotional exercises'. They're buying the outputs of your work: 'streamlined processes', 'productive warehouses' and 'increased confidence'. They buy whatever their objectives are.

That's why your proposal should describe the objectives, outcomes and benefits first, and your approach and methodology second.

Describe your approach and methodology in enough detail that the client understands what you're going to do and how you're going to work with them. Articulate how you're going to get the client from 'here' to 'there'. Map out their journey: "Dear client, you are here, and that is where you want to get to. This is how we're going to get you there." Give an overview of the phases and provide detail on the steps within each phase.

Some people use the terms 'approach' and 'methodology' interchangeably, but they are different. The methodology is the tool, technique, framework or method you use to facilitate the assignment. Your approach is how you work, interact and engage with the client. The methodology describes what you will do, whereas the approach represents how you'll go about it.

The section on methodology in your proposal should cover three main topics:

A description of the methodologies

Why you believe these are the most suitable

The sequence in which you plan to use them

One paragraph for each will suffice. There's no need to demonstrate how much you know about the subject, as you've already constructed your credibility enough to win the client's trust. Provide them with a general appreciation, giving enough detail so they understand and can tell others what's going to happen.

Be specific and avoid using general terms. For example, if you're a productivity expert, don't propose 'problem-solving' as a method. Problem-solving is what you hope to achieve—your job here is to define the methods you're going to use to solve the problem. This might be Toyota's root cause analysis, Pareto's 80/20 reasoning or Ford's 8D method.

If you're an executive coach, don't say you're going to use 'coaching conversations' to help the client achieve their goal. Explain that you're going to use the GROW model, or the science of NLP, or perhaps the Appreciative Inquiry process.

Whichever method you select, be specific, succinct and accurate in your description. It's also worth including a simple diagram as it helps reduce the amount of text within the document. Don't make the chart too complicated though, as it will raise more questions than it answers, which could delay you winning the work.

Your approach is about how you work, interact and engage with the client. It will depend on four things:

How you best work with clients

How your client works best with you

The client's objectives

The amount of time you've budgeted

The first, and most obvious, is how you best work with clients. Do you immerse yourself into their environment or keep a professional but objective distance? Or maybe you have a more arms-length approach? You know how you work best. Tell the client what that is.

The client will also have a preferred way of working. They might need close, personal support. Or they might prefer to keep your meetings formal. They might want to communicate through email, sending you information before asking you to analyse or process it and send it back to them with a report. Listen to the client to understand their preferred way of working, and hopefully it will match yours. If it doesn't, they might not be your model client.

Your client's objectives and targets will have a significant influence on your approach. Imagine that your assignment is to perform an organisation structure analysis to reduce the number of employees and therefore reduce costs. It wouldn't go well if you were to adopt an 'engaged' approach and asked the staff who should be made redundant. Can you imagine the chaos that would ensue? In this case, the best approach would be data driven. The analysis would be conducted by a small team of a trusted few within the client's organisation.

If on the other hand your brief was to implement a new working practice, you'd need to adopt a consultative and inclusive approach. Taking a hands-off approach wouldn't work, as the changes wouldn't be socialised within the company. The staff would reject the changes or not understand why they were being implemented.

An individual client wanting to improve their confidence

would require a supporting and reassuring approach. Someone who employs a personal coach to improve their sporting prowess might prefer someone who pushes them to their limits.

Your approach will also be influenced by how much time you can spend with the client. Spending time with a client allows the assignment to 'breathe', creating space for relationships to deepen. If the time is restricted, the focus is more functional, concentrating on checking progress and moving on to the next phase of their journey.

Step 6—Provide The Options

Providing a range of options in your proposal puts the odds in your favour. Proposing a single solution gives the client just two choices—either they decide to accept the proposal or not—giving you a 50/50 chance of winning the work.

However, if you propose four options, the odds shift in your favour 4/1. There are four choices to say "yes" and just one to say "no", which is a far better position to be in.

The options you propose must all be able to satisfy the client's requirements but offer different levels of support. Make Option A the most basic of your offers. It will involve the least amount of direct assistance but still satisfy your client's requirements. Then offer options B, C and D at increasing levels of support, accompanied of course by an increasing cost. Here's a simplified example:

Option A: Three monthly coaching sessions, each lasting two hours.

Option B: Four monthly coaching sessions, each lasting two hours, plus six months' access to an online learning resource.

Option C: Six monthly coaching sessions, each lasting three hours, plus six months' access to an online learning resource plus lifetime membership of a Facebook support group of like-minded people.

Option D: Twelve monthly coaching sessions, each lasting three hours, plus twelve months' access to an online learning resource plus lifetime membership of a Facebook support group of like-minded people.

Option A would be the minimum required to achieve client outcomes. However, the client is most likely to choose one of the higher-priced options due to the additional levels of service. When was the last time you were given a wine list at a restaurant? Which bottle did you choose? Very few people pick the cheapest. Most will choose a mid-priced bottle, while some will go for the most expensive. The same is true for your proposals. Don't be afraid to have an option in your proposal that gives good service at a reasonable cost. If you offer a few other higher-priced options that provide more value, the client is most likely to choose one of those.

Step 7—Establish The Timescales

Your proposal should give an estimation of how long the assignment will take. This doesn't need to be a detailed project plan identifying each activity, but it does need to provide an overview and give enough detail for the reader to understand what you will do and in which sequence.

You'd be mistaken to think that giving a detailed project plan in the proposal will make a good impression. The unnecessary information will raise questions as there is more for the client to understand. Too much information could also give away your 'secret sauce', the information you're trying to sell. If you tell them in detail what you're going to do and how you're going to do it, what's to stop the client from simply doing it themselves?

As underhand as this might be, some clients might just be using your proposal to get information and have no intention to buy your services.

Too much detail will also reveal the timing and therefore the cost of the assignment. For example, a proposal offering a service priced at £100,000 might show in the accompanying project plan that this will take you 50 hours. A client with a 'time-for-money' mindset will soon work out that they're paying you £2,000 per hour. It won't matter that you're giving them excellent value for money based on a high ROI—most clients will find a rate of £2,000 per hour a difficult pill to swallow.

Another reason not to give too much detail in your proposals is that it's impossible to see into the future, so don't make firm commitments about dates and timings unless you need to. When defining timescales use words such as 'estimated' and 'expected'. By using phrases like 'commit', 'deadline' or 'completed by the latest' you could be agreeing to something that's out of your control.

Of course, there will be occasions when a client holds you to a fixed completion date. They may have their own deadlines, so if a client makes it clear that hitting a target completion date is important then you'll need to agree to it. In these cases, you could ask for a bonus payment if the target is achieved. That way, if you do need to spend more time on achieving it, the additional costs will be covered.

Step 8—Agree On Accountabilities

The nature of consulting and coaching means it's a participation sport—you cannot be accountable for everything. So, make clear in your proposal who is responsible for what.

It's essential to talk this through from the outset, so introduce the subject during your conversations with the client and make sure they understand what they're committing to. Don't wait till you prepare your proposal to set them out. Remember: your proposal should contain no surprises—it's to formalise and confirm what has already been agreed.

The amount of client interaction required will vary depending on your service and the assignment outcomes. Coaches and consultants are accountable for providing the methodology, skills and experience to facilitate the changes required. They're also responsible for achieving the outputs—after all, that's why the client hired you.

There will be some things you'll need the client to do if the assignment is to be a success. You can't be expected to achieve the outcomes if the client doesn't engage in the process or doesn't provide you with everything you need to facilitate the change.

Agreeing accountabilities might be as simple as asking the client to attend all meetings on time or to provide data, or perhaps to get stakeholders involved in the communications to the broader workforce. Whatever they are, the proposal needs to make them clear.

Including the accountabilities in your proposal in black and white helps set the tone of the assignment. It emphasises the message "We're in the same boat and need to row it together." But remember: if the client holds up their end of the bargain and performs their tasks, you are accountable for delivering the outputs. The buck stops with you—this is what you're being paid for.

Step 9—Get The Authorisation

This section of your document is standard, so it can be used in any of your proposals. It consists of a statement that confirms the chosen option and a place for both parties to sign. Once signed, this turns your proposal into a formal legal agreement, giving you the authority to proceed. This is the format I tend to use:

Agreement

The client has chosen to proceed with option _____ as described in this proposal.

Work will start on the date of _____

The Company and the Client accept and agree this signed proposal forms a legal contract. The client has read and agrees to the Company's General Terms and Conditions in Appendix 1 of this document.

The Company
Signed _____
Print Name _____
Date _____

The Client
Signed _____
Print Name _____
Date _____

There have been a few times I have been tempted to start work before the client signs the agreement. Every time I have done so, the assignment has been a flop. In my experience, if the client is slow in signing the agreement, you can take it as a warning sign that something is wrong.

A standard set of your terms and conditions must also be included—I place these in the appendix and reference them in the agreement. The trick is to make sure they are robust enough to safeguard you and your company while not being too complicated or too long. They must be written in plain English and be easy to understand.

The more complex and lengthy the terms and conditions, the more tempted the client will be to get legal advice. This will lead to questions being raised and requests for changes to be made. Additional legal activity will frustrate both parties and extend the time it takes to get the proposal signed off. In turn, there will be a delay in starting the work and sending your invoices.

I recommend you hire a commercial law expert to help create a standard set of terms and conditions. Don't perform an internet search and copy and paste text found on a random website, no matter how impressive and official it might look. Sit down with a real person who is an expert in this field and draft your own set of general terms and conditions.

Step 10—Check The Document

It's taken months of discussions and you've lost count of the number of cups of coffee consumed during meetings. But you're almost there. You've constructed credibility, built relationships and the client has asked for a proposal. The last thing you want to happen now is to undo all the hard work. Everything you've established will unravel if you hand over a poorly written proposal.

Proofread the document to check your work for errors in punctuation, spelling or grammar. It might sound simple, but it can be difficult. When you read your writing, your eye sometimes sees what you should have written rather than what's on the page. This means you need to find different ways of spotting the errors in your writing. Read the proposal through aloud. If it doesn't sound right, chances are it's not written right.

Coaches and consultants love three-letter acronyms (TLAs). VSA, KPI, ABC, ROI, OSA, PAA—we simply can't get enough of them. Remember that your client might not share your enthusiasm. Try not to make your proposal sound like secret code. Check that wherever you've used an acronym you've accompanied it by an explanation of what it stands for.

I also find that consultants love to write in the passive voice.

This is where the subject in the sentence is acted upon; they receive the action expressed by the verb. I'm not trying to be a member of the grammar police, but overuse of passive voice in a proposal can make it flat and uninteresting. You don't want your client to be bored when reading your document. Aim to turn passive phrases into active ones.

Watch out for the word 'by' as a clue. For example:

Passive: "The delivery of services has been stopped by a machine breaking down."

Active: "A machine breaking down stopped the delivery of services."

Consider hiring a professional proofreader if you're not confident in your writing skills. Even better, find a writing coach to teach you how to proofread.

You're ready. The proposal is written, the client is expecting it and it confirms what you've already agreed. It's logical and connects with them at an emotional level. They believe in you, your approach and your ability to help them. Lastly, it makes sound financial sense to invest in your services.

Now send the document to them and get yourself ready to win the work.

❋ ❋ ❋

Ten Steps To Prepare Proposals

    Step 1—Demonstrate you understand
    Step 2—State the objectives
    Step 3—Set the targets

Step 4—Quantify financial benefits
Step 5—Describe the methodology
Step 6—Provide the options
Step 7—Establish the timescales
Step 8—Agree on accountabilities
Step 9—Get the authorisation
Step 10—Check the document

WINNING WORK

What

Encourage and persuade your future client to step over the line and say "yes" to working with you.

Why

People do not like being sold to, and their default position is either to defer a decision or say "no". So, sometimes they need a little persuasion to sign on the dotted line. You want the client to feel comfortable and confident enough to say "yes" without being pushed or manipulated.

How

Think like a salesperson by preparing well for every sales meeting. During the meetings, surface and remove reasons that could be holding the client back from buying.

※ ※ ※

In *Glengarry Glen Ross*, Alec Baldwin plays an aggressive representative from the corporate office who's brought in to motivate a group of real estate agents. Here's one of his infamous 'motivational' speeches:

"You can't play in the man's game, you can't close them—go home and tell your wife your troubles. Because only one thing counts in this life: Get them to sign on the line which is dotted. You hear me, you ******s? A-B-C. A-Always, B-Be, C-Closing. Always be closing. ALWAYS BE CLOSING."

This speech results in the salespeople resorting to a host of unethical tactics to achieve their sales numbers. And all because they've been told to Always Be Closing.

I tear my hair out when I hear someone repeat that phrase. There's a time and place to have a sales conversation, and the last thing you should try to do is close the deal at every opportunity. If you try too soon, the client will simply walk away.

The best time to win the work is a day or two after the client has read your proposal. But don't be tempted to morph from a considerate service professional into a pushy, aggressive salesperson. The client will be confused by the change of personality.

You do, however, need to have a direct sales discussion to get the client to sign off your proposal. It's possible to be persuasive without being a prat.

Step 1—Believe In Yourself

If you want to win work, you must believe that what you do will help the client and be able to transfer that belief to them. If you want somebody to sign up and you don't radiate that belief, the client will see your doubt as plain as day. Some unscrupulous coaches and consultants will try to manipulate or pressure a client into buying a service they don't have experience or belief in. If you do this, your business will have a short shelf life.

You need to have experienced, taught and believe in what you offer. If you're going to get more clients, you need to be convinced of and committed to your service offering. Believers sell. If you don't believe, you're sure to fail. But it's not enough just to believe. To sell your services, you need to be able to transfer that belief to your client, as most people are more convinced by the transfer of emotion than the technical and theoretical aspects of your proposal.

You need to have an internal conviction that you're an expert in your field and that you have an approach clients can use. If you don't believe in yourself, why should the client? Your conviction needs to be such that you cannot understand why clients would *not* buy your services. You need to believe the client is missing out on something they would benefit from. If you don't, you'll struggle to speak with enthusiasm and authenticity, and the client will pick up on it.

Step 2—Identify Their Style

You'll encounter a range of personality types when selling your services. It's therefore essential to identify each potential client's individual profile and plan your meeting to suit. Here are some examples of personality types:

The Zombie

This person, as the name suggests, is the kind you want to avoid. They are never going to hire you, no matter how great you are. They get you in a funk, are often pessimistic, cynical, unimpressed and are not interested in their own development. This client has too many challenges, both in their professional and personal life, and their problems weigh them down so much that they can't look up to see how much you can help them.

Unless these are the traits you identified in your model clients I recommend you stay away from this person.

The Achiever

This person is the opposite of a Zombie and knows what they

want. They'll be able to see the outcomes of your support and how it will benefit them and will have already have a clear idea of how much they are willing to pay. If your service aligns with their requirements and your personalities resonate, they will buy after one or two meetings. You won't come across this type of client often. So, when you do, grab on to them.

A word of warning, however: don't try to sell them something they don't want or need. If you do, they'll walk away, as this client knows what they want and will find someone else to avoid being delayed. Their heart and head are already set on the action, and they know the support they want.

The Computer

This person is task-orientated but introverted, so they're concerned about the individual components of your services. They'll be judging you on the quality and exactness of your responses, so the best way to deal with them is to slow down, match their pace and style and be clear cut and literal with them.

The more structure and detail you give, the more their confidence in you will grow. Tell the client how your service works, the steps in the process and how the outcomes are derived. The benefits you quote need to be quantifiable and demonstrable; these guys are all about the detail.

They need a lot of information before deciding to buy, so their buying cycle tends to be quite long—don't expect a quick sale. They need to analyse all the data and reflect on what you've told them. Where an Achiever or a Director will need one or two touchpoints, a Computer will need many. They'll often come back to you several times with lots of questions and points for clarification. It won't serve you well to try to accelerate the sale. They need to be convinced they're choosing the right provider before committing.

The Director

This person is also task-orientated, direct and impatient and wants to get to the crux of the matter straight away. They won't beat around the bush and will want to know everything about you and your service: who you are, what services you provide, the benefits they bring, how long it takes to achieve them and how much it will cost.

You need to be direct and precise with them, and if you are, they'll move quickly. Get straight to the point. Standardised services with a fixed price work well with this type of client.

Don't try to build rapport with a Director. At this point in their journey, they're too driven and preoccupied to bother with niceties. They know what they want and what they require from you, and they'll want to start as soon as possible. The clearer you are with the benefits of your service, the faster they will buy.

The Worrier

These people tend to be a little quiet but like to build strong relationships. So, as with the Computer, you'll need to move at a pace they're comfortable with. Worriers are sensitive souls and they care what other people think about them, including how people might react to their decision to hire you. They often need reassurance from you and will talk it through with others before signing on the dotted line.

Your approach should be to try to empathise with them, reassure that you're a good match and that you're confident you'll work together well. Emphasise the upsides and downplay the dangers. The more you talk, the more comfortable they will get. Listen and give them your full attention, building a strong and trusting relationship before making a sales offer.

If you propose working together too soon, Worriers will run a mile. Help them feel comfortable and they'll feel confident enough to step over the line. When the time is right to make a sales offer, start with a low- or no-cost offer with little perceived risk for them, then build the size of the assignment as their trust in you grows.

The Socialite

As the name suggests, these people tend to be extroverts and highly sociable. They love to collaborate and thrive when working on large projects that require people to work together on a common cause. They sit somewhere between the Computer and the Worrier concerning working style and love getting stuff done. They have an equal focus on themselves and others. They'll talk about their past achievements, their present concerns and their future ambitions, and will listen and learn about what you do.

Socialites have a habit of making commitments a little too quickly, then forgetting what they've agreed. Don't be surprised if you have a different understanding of what was said and agreed to at a previous meeting. This happens a lot, especially when you arrive with a proposal in hand.

The best way to manage Socialites is to take notes at your meeting, write them up and email them a copy the same or following day. Use written communication to make sure you're both on the same page and have an aligned understanding of what was said.

Step 3—Visualise The Meeting

It's not just good practice to be prepared for each sales meeting—it's essential. I've found the best way to do this is to start with the end in mind. Visualise your meeting beforehand, imagine shaking hands with the client and winning the work, and then look in the rear-view mirror to see what happened to get you to that position. In your visualisation, how did you ask for the business? What specific words did you use?

Then visualise the steps before you asked for the work: was the client briefed, did they understand your proposal, and did they trust and believe in you? Then think back further to the first time you came into contact with the client. What did you say and do that got the client to the point of asking for your help and support?

Using this visualisation technique before your next sales meeting can help you to understand the things you've said and done before to win work. I've found the following six sets of questions useful to ask as part of your preparation.

Set 1

Do I get it? Do I understand my client's current position, their challenges and ambitions? Do I know with absolute certainty what they want and need?

Do they get it? Do they understand that without my help, their current situation will not change for the better?

Set 2

Is this right for me? Will taking this person on as a client enhance or tarnish my reputation and credibility?

Is this right for them? Is my service and support the best option for the client? Is my proposed assignment suitable for their situation and personality?

Set 3

Am I confident? Will the work generate the outcomes and benefits the client is looking for?

Are they confident? Will the work generate the outcomes and benefits the client is looking for?

Set 4

Am I ready to jump? Do I know what I am getting myself into? Have I weighed up the benefits and risks to me?

Are they ready to jump? Do they know what they are getting themselves into? Have I made clear, and do they understand what is required from both of us and the process we are going to follow?

Set 5

Do I trust them? Do I believe they have been open and honest with me?

Do they trust me? Have I taken the effort and time to construct enough credibility so there are no lingering doubts?

Set 6

Do I like them? Does the thought of working with this client over the next few weeks and months fill me with anticipation and joy, or anxiety and despair?

Do they like me? Have they answered their phone when I call and responded to emails quickly? Has the tone of their voice and written messages been friendly and open?

If the answers to these questions are "yes", then you're in a superb position to push on with your sales meeting. If you've answered a few with "no", then you should think through what needs to be done or said to turn them into "yes".

Step 4—Plan The Conversation

All the way through my career as a consultant, every time I met a potential client I would receive a call thirty minutes later from whoever was my boss at the time: "Did you get the work?" or "Are you going to send them a proposal?" They all had a short-term view of that month's performance. If I wasn't on a fee-earning day, there had better be a good reason for it.

But the reality of sales is that rarely will you meet someone for the first time and they will ask to become your client. In most situations, you'll spend several months establishing and building your credibility and understanding the client's requirements. You'll send them your information products and have several conversations. Following that, you'll prepare and deliver a proposal to them. Then they'll love your plan and will want to meet to finalise the details.

It's this 'closing' sales conversation that contains the action my old bosses were looking for. You only get one chance at it, so you would do well to plan it out rather than just turning up and flying by the seat of your pants. It might have taken you six months or even a year to get your client to this point. Do not drop the ball now.

All sales meetings need to be planned, whether you're proposing a small introductory piece of work for £5,000 or a significant transformation programme for £5million. Follow a set framework, so you always arrive prepared and give yourself the best possible chance of winning the work. To do this, grab a notebook and a pen, then write each of the headings below on a separate page.

What do I want?

The obvious answer here is to win the work. But although it's obvious, you'd be surprised how many people wander into a sales meeting without setting clear targets. If you haven't set your desired outcomes, there's not much point turning up for the meeting. Decide what and how much you want to get.

What do they want?

Go back and reread your proposal. It should articulate the client's requirements, so read it and reread it until you can recite it without needing to refer to the document. Decide the five most important points and write them down.

What have I proposed?

Keeping your proposal at hand, memorise what you've said you will do and your justifications for doing it. Your proposal will have a range of options. Which will serve your client best and provide the most value? Write a bullet point for each option and put an asterisk next to the preferred option.

What are my strengths?

When you start the sales meeting, there will be things that work in your favour and things that work against you. My preference is to focus on the positives and not the negative. Thinking through your strengths will allow you to walk into that meeting confident and ready to handle both complements and objections. If you focus on your weaknesses, you'll have lost the sale before the meeting starts.

Start to note your strengths for this particular client. These could include having a great relationship with the client's boss, so that they feel obligated to say "yes", or perhaps you've worked together before on a different project. Of course, you'll have the additional advantage of having built trust and credibility with them.

What needs to be done?

This is a simple 'to-do' list to identify the preparatory activities you need to complete. It should cover both tangible and intangible tasks. These might include memorising your proposal, planning the structure of the conversation, defining the specific words you will use to ask for the business, printing two or three copies of the document and booking a quiet table in a nice restaurant to have the meeting.

When it comes to sales meetings, surprises are not a good thing. Plan your meeting well and make sure you have everything organised beforehand so you can glide into a meeting and waltz out with a signed order for work.

Step 5—Brace For Objections

The sales coach Brian Tracey said, "There are no sales without objections." He was right: objections to your offer usually indicate your client is interested. Treat them like the GPS guidance instructions you get while you drive; they will lead the way to your final destination of closing the sale. If there are no objections, there is no interest, and no interest means there is no sale.

So, when a potential client raises an objection, remember that most of the time they haven't ruled out working with you. Quite the opposite—they just need more information and encouragement to make a commitment.

There are thousands of concerns that clients can and do raise when being sold consulting and coaching. But I believe they can be grouped into six basic themes:

"It's too expensive"

This is the most frequent objection you will hear when clients hesitate to buy your service. It's usually raised about two-thirds of the way through the sales conversation, and you'll recognise it when they start to ask questions about cost and your terms and conditions. I've found that when a client says "price", "costs", or "expensive", they really mean "value". They simply don't believe they'll see enough benefit compared to your price;

in short, the perceived ROI is too low.

Most clients do not look to work with the cheapest coach or consultant as deep down they know they'll get what they pay for. If a consultant is charging well below the standard market rate, the client will worry there is an unsavoury reason for it. Most clients look to pay a fair price, not the lowest price.

At this point, it's too late in the sales process to retrace your steps and propose an alternative service. It's also too late to offer a substantial discount. Small reductions are okay, but not large ones. If you do, your credibility will nosedive, and you'll lose the client's respect. The assignment will start on the wrong footing, and you'll not be considered an equal partner.

The best option is to reassure the client that your service will deliver what they want to achieve. Remind them of the primary benefit, how it will address their challenges and achieve their ambitions. Once you've said this, pause for a few seconds to let it sink in, and then tell them they're getting a good deal. And if they look at the proposal in its totality, they'll be delighted with your support and the outcomes you can give them.

"I'm not sure it will work"

This form of opposition is aimed at the service and solution you have proposed and the expected outcomes you have stated. The client doesn't believe that what you're offering will achieve the forecast benefits.

There are five things you need to do and say if a client raises a point like this. First, ask them what specific element of your proposed solution is causing concern. Second, quickly, and I mean immediately after the client stops speaking, recap the structure of your service, paying particular attention to how your approach will mitigate that concern. Third, after your recap, make a crystal clear statement: your work will satisfy all of the requirements.

Fourth, provide testimonials that prove you have a strong track record of completing successful assignments just like theirs and how satisfied previous clients have been. Last, summarise and assure the client that your service will do exactly what it says on the tin and give them the benefits you've committed to achieving.

"I can do it by myself"

Sometimes the client's pride can get in the way of making the right decision to hire you. You will spot this when they try to impress you and demonstrate how much they know about the topic. The ego can be a terrible thing that nobody is immune to, and it's the downfall of many a successful business person.

The client might start to talk over you, articulating complex and detailed viewpoints and asking convoluted, obscure questions about your approach. You might see this as the client showing interest by asking lots of questions, but whereas asking relevant questions is good, irrelevant ones are not. When you sense the client is 'showboating' like this, always take the moral high ground. Tell them how inspired you are by working with somebody who already knows so much about the subject, and that they can take it to the next level by working with you.

People with big egos like to talk and be listened to, so allow them to do just that. Let them talk, make sure you listen and allow them to feel important. All this listening will endear you to them, but never allow them to assume the position of the expert. They might know a lot, but make sure they're aware that you know far more, or you will lose their respect.

"One more question"

When your client says this, hold on to your hat and get ready to answer a long list of questions, not just one. Cautious clients will ask lots of questions to delay making a decision, so remember that you are the person who knows more about your services than anyone else in the world.

When your client starts to ask relevant questions to clarify how you would work together, you're in an excellent position to ask for the sale. Demonstrate your expertise by thanking them for the question and answering it as fully and confidently as possible. After you've provided an answer, circle back and check with them that you've adequately responded. When the rate of questions slows, ask if there's anything else they need to know. If there's not, now is the right time to ask for the business.

"I don't like you"

Now, almost nobody is going to say this, but you might get a sense that the two of you are not getting on. You need to establish if this is a pattern or unusual behaviour. Sometimes people can be a bit grumpy and can have their off days; I'm sure we've all been a bit sharp to someone who didn't deserve it.

Some days a client might have had a bad day and they're sitting across a desk from you and there you are talking to complete your sale. As much as they want and need your services, today is not the day for them to say "yes" to anything. It is not your fault or theirs, it's just the way things are at that specific time.

If this is the case, you'll notice that they seem more negative than usual and behave differently. They might criticise your proposal where before they were complimentary about it and liked your solution. Try not to take these situations to heart. The client might be venting their frustrations on you, and the reality is that you're unlikely to be the cause of their demeanour.

You might feel a little shaken and confused by their outburst, but don't let it get to you. Sometimes this is easier said than done. The best thing to do is remember is that it's not personal, it's about other things that are happening in the client's life. Remain calm, don't show you've been affected and stay polite and professional. Your positive and reassuring behaviour will highlight to the client how poorly they are behaving. Their negativity will subside, often they will apologise and then open up about the real cause of their frustration. To coin the British phrase, "Keep calm and carry on"—it's not you, it's them.

If, however, they show this antagonistic attitude again, you will do well to ask yourself if this person is your model client and whether you really will enjoy working with them on a long project.

"...................."

We've run through some of the everyday things clients say to delay or avoid buying your services. However, perhaps the most common form of objection is the one that remains unspoken. This is where the client has concerns or doesn't understand an element of your proposal but says nothing. Most of the time, they will sit quite still, almost frozen, trying to hide their discomfort. When they freeze their speech patterns will also slow and perhaps even stop altogether.

If someone goes quiet on you, ask them an open question and then say nothing until they respond, even if this creates an awkward silence. Just wait until they answer. Then listen to the answer—you want to understand what might be holding them back. Then continue to ask open questions until they tell you what is bothering them and stopping them from progressing.

Step 6—Be A Salesperson

What are the traits of a good salesperson? Grab a pen and some paper and write a list of all the desirable mental and physical attributes a top-notch seller has. Now take that list, crumple it into a ball and throw it in the bin. Listen to me when I say: the number one trait you need to think like a salesperson is to be yourself. Do not try to be somebody you're not or would like to be.

If you want to sell your services, grow your business and enjoy the adventure, you need to be yourself. Show the world who you are—it's the best way to get clients. To think like a salesperson is simply to be yourself. The biggest mistake you can make as a coach or consultant is to imitate what you think a good salesperson says and does. Failing to talk the way you talk, act the way you do and look the way you look will not serve you well and in the long run will lose you clients. Be yourself.

Don't let self-doubt creep in or allow insecurities to fill your mind. Do not compare yourself to others. You may not have the same services, expertise, personality or experience that other coaches or consultants offer, but that's a good thing. Be yourself and play to your strengths.

I was born and brought up in Scotland and therefore have a strong Scottish accent. I feared clients in London and other countries wouldn't take me seriously as I didn't have a 'posh' accent. So, I practised talking with an English accent and even considered taking elocution lessons. I must say it turned out horribly. In my naive attempts to be like them, clients thought I was making fun of their accent. Be yourself.

A lot of coaches and consultants forget they're service professionals. In this industry, it's challenging to be successful if you're not confident and don't believe in yourself. Clients can smell nervousness a mile away. Being a little shy and nervous might be endearing if you're a child, or even if you're on a first date. But it has no place in the world of coaching and consulting. This is a high-trust profession, and your clients need your guidance and look to you for the answers. You're the steady, confident expert providing the support they need. Good salespeople are confident.

Be positive, visualise what you want and work hard to get it. Positive thinking will not make you a superhero who can do anything. But it will allow you to do the important stuff better than negative thinking would. Your outlook on life, your clients, your family—in fact, everything you do—is controlled by what goes on in your mind.

In the book *Secrets of Closing the Sale*, Zig Ziglar says:

Your business is never really good or bad 'out there.' Your business is either good or bad right between your own two ears.

Thinking like a salesperson also requires you to remember that you are there to sell. When I was first sent out to sell consulting services, I didn't know what to say. I would jabber on so there were no awkward gaps and continue to talk through the meeting without ever getting round to asking for the business. I would end up being seen as a professional visiting friend, rather than a service professional they would benefit from working with. The sales meetings would wind down and drift off without me having made a concerted effort to close the sale. The client and I would go our separate ways thinking that it was a nice to catch up, but it was a waste of each other's time.

To get the business, you need to ask for it. But there's no point asking for the work if you have the wrong attitude towards the client. Be honest with yourself before each meeting. How do you view the client? Do you see them as somebody you can overcharge, make money from and then disappear, or are they someone with a set of challenges and ambitions you can help with? Is your priority to make the sale and be the primary beneficiary or is it to make the client the main recipient of the benefits?

Salespeople who focus on themselves tend to have short careers. Those who focus on helping the customer tend to get repeat business, a strong reputation and longevity. You're a service professional, you're in the service industry. Your profession is to help others and not yourself.

The client regards a service professional as a person who is driven to help them while promoting their service. Adopting a balanced approach encourages the client to open up and talk more freely. They'll know you're trying to help them through the your services and that you'll make them a fair offer.

Step 7—Avoid these things

When I started my consulting career, I 'shadowed' senior consultants and partners of the firm I worked for to observe them and learn how to sell consulting services. Some were fantastic, while others were poor. I often wondered how these consultants had managed to get such a senior position while being so bad at selling.

Being the diligent young consultant I was, I wrote copious notes on what I observed to learn what did and didn't work. When I reviewed my records, there were striking similarities between the meetings that didn't result in a sale. Once I noticed this, I began to be able to tell even when people were shaking hands at the start of the meeting whether it was going to result in new work. I would watch the senior consultant from my firm and know they were about to make a mess of it. I also knew that, as the junior consultant, there was nothing I could do to intervene.

The mistakes I saw consultants make in conversation were about as obvious as Big Ben from Westminster bridge. But the senior partner who was leading the shambles of a sales conversation just couldn't see it. They were oblivious that many months of hard work were being destroyed in those first few minutes.

When sales meetings die, they rarely go out with a bang. They fizzle and whimper, like a damp firework that fails to sparkle. Irrespective of whether the senior consultant made a big mistake or a small one, if they'd realised what was happening they could have changed course. One of my first observations was that a lack of preparation kills the meeting before it's even started. It makes it near impossible to hold a productive sales conversation, as whenever you talk from a position of being unprepared, every word you utter screams of unprofessionalism.

Another big mistake is to be late for a meeting. This includes forgetting meetings, being double-booked or prioritising another client and rescheduling. All of these will put you at a disadvantage. In a similar vein, the words you use can demonstrate a lack of professionalism. That includes bad language and talking about a sensitive subject such as sex, religion or politics.

Professionalism is also reflected by what you wear. Too casual and you might not be respected; too formal and the client might not be able to relate to you. I like the 'plus one' approach to clothing, that is, dressing slightly smarter than the client does. If the client wears jeans and a t-shirt, you wear chinos and a polo shirt, or relaxed trousers and a casual shirt. If the clients wear formal trousers and an open-necked shirt, you wear a suit and tie, or a formal dress and jacket. But only dress 'plus one'—do not make the gap too big. If you were to go 'plus two,' i.e. they wear jeans and you wear a suit, you might not resonate with them on a personal level.

Some sales books and courses advise you to take an adversarial and challenging position. This is not an approach that will build trusting and respectful relationships. If you were the client, who would you want to work with: an abrasive and confrontational coach, or someone who knows their stuff, brings a lot of value and you would enjoy spending time with?

It's important to remember that your client might not be the only person in the company's purchasing procedure. It's essential to identify the key stakeholders and find out the part they play in the process. I've seen consultants have a string of meetings with the client only to have them turn up to the closing meeting with three additional people who need to sign off on the deal. The client needed their authorisation but hadn't involved them in the scoping and shaping of the proposal, so they didn't understand the problem they were trying to solve or even who the consultant was. The whole process was reset back to zero, and it took another six months to submit another proposal.

The longer it takes for a doctor to diagnose a medical condition, the harder it becomes to treat. The longer it takes for a police detective to find evidence, the less likely the crime is to be solved. The same holds true for selling coaching and consulting.

The longer it takes to move from the initial scoping meeting to the final sales meeting, the longer the odds of winning the work. As the dwell time increases, new challenges will come into the client's life and require his attention, meaning that your sale will lose momentum.

Sometimes a client might view you as an employee and want you to be subservient to them. While you are clearly there to provide a service, that does not make them more senior to you. Stay professional and remember you're the expert. You'll sense when a client has this attitude during the sales discussion. Does it feel more like a job interview or an exciting, collaborative meeting? If the meeting goes down the route of the former, don't fall into the trap of acting subserviently to try to win the work. But don't take the opposite approach either, adopting an arrogant approach to redress the imbalance of power. Neither of these behaviours works well, either in the short term or the long term.

Try to stop your sales conversations from taking the scenic route. Consultants who are inexperienced in selling their services often feel more comfortable making small talk than asking for the work, and they convince themselves they are creating rapport. While building rapport is essential, if your discussion meanders and rambles on for too long or at the wrong point, it can undo the sale. Stay on target and stick to the subject at hand, which is always how you can help the client.

Many coaches and consultants are uncomfortable talking about money. Why is it that one coach charges £50 an hour and another sets their fees at £500 per hour? One might be more qualified or have a more impressive list of clients but, assuming they offer the same service, is one coach really ten times better than the other? Often the only difference is that the cheaper coach suffers from 'money discomfort'. This can be a debilitating condition, and it has two causes: 'general money syndrome' and 'money vertigo'. The first is a general discomfort when talking about money and fees in any form, and the second is an increasing level of discomfort the higher the fees become.

In both cases, your discomfort will raise questions and doubt in the buyer's mind. Somebody without this affliction names their price—they know their value and are comfortable enough for their price to reflect it. The consultant who suffers from money discomfort, however, will often say something like, "Sure… uhh… well… what I'm asking might sound a lot… but… umm… I will be doing a lot of work… and it will take a lot of time… I was thinking about… £30,000? Is that too expensive? If it is, I could reduce it." Compare this to what someone with money confidence would say: "My fees will be between £50,000 and £55,000."

If you have general money syndrome or money vertigo, your client will start to question your credibility. They'll wonder if you're worth the fee and what could be the reasons for your apparent discomfort. They'll think, "That is a bit cheap. I wonder why? Are we too big and complex for them? We might be better going to a larger firm for coaching." And if you do manage to scrape by, at best they'll think, "I like this coach, but I think I can negotiate their fees down—a lot."

Money discomfort is contagious. Don't let your client come in close contact with it or they'll catch it from you, causing a whole new set of problems.

Step 8—Empathise, Don't Sympathise

There are three stages of approval a client goes through when buying professional services:

I believe you
I like you
I buy you

In the consulting and coaching arena, the client first and foremost buys you. Yes, you'll need to have the right processes and methodologies in place, but it will always boil down to if they believe and like you, and if your proposition presents itself as an investable opportunity.

To win work, the single biggest skill you can have is the ability to empathise. It's empathy that oils the shifting of the client's perception of you from believing to liking, and then to buying.

When a potential client asks to meet you to talk about how you might be able to help them, they're already starting to believe you. Otherwise they wouldn't have asked to meet you in the first place. You've taken the time to construct your credibility and the client is willing to meet you to establish if they believe in you. They want to be convinced that you are everything you've made yourself out to be. The way they'll do that is to look you in the eyes to gauge if you're the real deal, that you're a genuine expert in your field and have an authentic work ethic.

However, being good at what you do and having good intentions for your client is not enough. They must also like you. They have to feel that you resonate with them and that you'll be able to work together productively and pleasurably.

Before you ask for the business, clients need to feel comfortable and confident in you. Many people use the terms 'empathy' and 'sympathy' interchangeably. However, there's a world of difference between them.

Let's start with the term 'sympathy'. The word is constructed of two parts: *sym* meaning together, and *pathos* meaning emotion. So the word 'sympathy' describes when one person shares the same emotions and feelings as another. Similarly, the term 'empathy' also consists of two parts: *em* and *pathos*. However, in this form, the *em* draws from the Greek for 'in'. So, the term 'empathy' means understanding how someone might feel, but without having these feelings yourself. Empathy implies more emotional distance than sympathy.

Sympathy is sharing
Empathy is understanding

For example, if people support the same football club, when

that club loses an important game they will sympathise with each other. They share the same disappointment. But if one person supports a different team, they'll empathise. They understand how it feels, but they don't share the same emotion at that time. In other words, we can understand another person's disappointment but not share it.

The reason I've gone into this detail is to warn you. The minute you start to sympathise with a client, you've lost the sale. They'll no longer view you as an adviser but as an equal, or even a friend. Empathy means that you remain emotionally detached from the client and their challenges, so you can be in a position to support them and propose suitable ways to help. In Zig Ziglar's book *Secrets of Closing the Deal*, he says.

> *You move from your side of the table to the prospect's side. Realistically that is where the sale is going to be made, and the chance of that happening is greatly increased because from his side of the table you can make your presentation from his point of view.*

Move to your client's side of the table to understand their perspective, yes. Put their shoes on and feel what they feel? No.

Step 9—Say The Price

You sense the client is interested in hiring you. However, before you ask for the business, you'll need to confirm the price. If done clumsily, this has the potential to become tricky, as it can open a host of excuses for them not to buy your services.

At this point in the sales process, the client should already know what you are going to charge. During your initial discussion, you will have given them a price range and later on specified the exact figure in your proposal.

They know the price, but sometimes when it's said out loud

it can still come as a shock. To avoid any potential adverse reaction, I tend to use a technique called the 'sandwich' close. It's a conversational framework that 'sandwiches' the price between two other pieces of positive information: what they're getting for their money and the outcomes of that investment. This approach consists of three parts: first, inputs, second, cost, and third, outputs. An example of a sandwich close might look something like this:

Start with the inputs:

"So, let me summarise. I propose we start with a ten-week assignment to fix the quality problem in your production facility. We'll use the first two weeks to analyse the data to pinpoint the root causes. The remaining eight weeks will be used to implement the countermeasures. I'll be in the factory four days a week over the full duration, and there'll also be a data analyst for the first two weeks."

Then move on to the price:

"The fee for the assignment is a fixed price of £120,000 and is inclusive of expenses. I expect to rectify your quality problem in eight weeks, but if it takes longer, it will be at my cost, not yours."

Now it's time to finish on the positive—the outputs:

"I expect to reduce your production defect rate down to less than 0.01%, which equates to an annual financial benefit of £950,000. The return on your investment in my services will be eightfold. To put it simply, you invest £120,000 in me, and ten weeks later I estimate we'll generate £950,000 for you. How does that sound to you?"

If the client responds positively, move to close the deal. If the client is not yet convinced, go on to describe the benefits that flow from the primary output. Use the 5 Es described in chapter three, Positioning Pricing, and chapter 6, Preparing Proposals, to articulate all the great things that will come from the assignment.

The sandwich close concludes with the outputs or benefits because they arouse the client's desire to purchase. Each time you state a benefit that's important to them, their desire grows. Watch their body language: if they show interest in a specific benefit you describe, then go into more detail to accentuate that point. If you articulate lots of benefits in quick succession, the client's desire accelerates to the point where they'll blurt out "Ok, I've heard enough, let's go for it, how soon can you start?"

To summarise, the sandwich close consists of the first piece of bread (the inputs), the filling (the price), and the second piece of bread (the outputs).

Step 10—Close The Deal

Sales can be tough. To maintain motivation, I find it helpful to remember three things. First, who gets the most benefit from the sale. Calculate the monetary value of your sales over the last 12 months and then calculate the financial value that your clients have gained over the same period. You'll find that your clients have probably gained 10 to 20 times more benefit than you. So, your clients get the most from your sales. You also win, but they get the better end of the deal. Feel good about selling your services to them—you're helping them deal with their challenges and achieve their ambitions, after all. They're lucky to be working with you.

Second, keep in mind that there's no such thing as a natural born salesperson. You don't need to be a cocky, outgoing 'people' person to be great at sales. Just be yourself.

I coach people to sell by being themselves—that's why I called my company Be Yourself Sales Coaching—and I hope this book gives you practical guidance on how to get more clients. But whichever sales approach you choose, the most important thing is to adapt it to suit your character and personality. Make it your own.

Last, and perhaps most important, if you want a successful and sustainable approach to getting more clients, you should remind yourself there's a big difference between refusal and rejection. When a client says "no", it's easy to let that create doubt in your 'salesperson' mind. Unless you believe in your abilities and that your service produces fantastic benefits, you might allow your enthusiasm and confidence to melt away.

My dog Bruno understands the difference between refusal and rejection. I'm never quite sure who is training who in our relationship, but it's clear that he doesn't accept the concept of rejection. When he asks for a treat (he does this by shaking his head side-to-side and shuffling backwards) and I say "no", he doesn't feel rejected. He just thinks that I didn't understand his request. He'll wait a minute or two, then come back to nudge me and signal again that he wants a treat. In his head, he's allowing me to correct my mistake. Come to think of it, I do think it's him who is training me.

The important lesson to understand from this is that, when a potential new client says "no" to you, be kind to them, just as Bruno is to me. Give them the benefit of the doubt and allow them to correct their mistake in not hiring you.

When a client declines your offer, adopt the mindset that it's their mistake, not yours. After all, you already know that your clients always get the better end of the deal. Be polite and patient and give them the chance to rectify their mistake and say "yes".

Sales books offer hundreds of routines to close the deal and encourage your client to say "yes". I consider the godfathers of sales to be Zig Ziglar and Brian Tracy, and I recommend that you read their books. Most set-piece closes originate from one of these two salesmen. But while they were giants in their field at one time, things have moved on, and in my opinion their work has dated badly.

I've researched and tried out hundreds of closing techniques and narrowed them down to a few favourites. For this book I've updated them and made them more relevant for today's service professionals. They've proven to be the most successful and suitable ways of closing the deal for coaches and consultants, so I've included them here.

The Boris Johnson Close

In 2016 Britain held a referendum to decide whether to stay in the European Union or not. Boris Johnson was already a leading political figure and his view of whether to 'leave' or 'remain' would have a significant influence on the outcome.

He decided to write two articles with opposing views, one listing the reasons to leave the EU and another with the reasons to stay. He already knew his preference was to go, so he made strong, convincing arguments in the 'leave' article and weaker ones in the 'remain' version. The 'leave' article was published and led the campaign to leave the EU. Johnson won.

You can adopt a similar approach when trying to close a deal with a new client. Talk them through both scenarios: what would happen if they decided to work with you and what would happen if they didn't. However, make sure the reasons the client should work with you are more convincing than the reasons for them to say no. Here's an example:

You: "So, we have covered a lot of ground, hopefully in enough detail that will enable you to make a decision to proceed. However, I do realise it's natural to think through all aspects of the work before making a decision. Would you find it useful if I were to summarise both the positive and negative elements of us working together?"

Client: "Yes, that would help me get everything straight in my mind."

You: "Ok, let's look at the negatives. It costs money to hire me, and I assume money is something you would like to hold on to. You are probably also concerned about the amount of work involved as you are already busy. Are these the two main ones?"

Client: "Yes, there are a few other minor points, but the big worries are time and money."

You: "Let's talk through the positives, the reasons why you should sign up for my services today. I understand you're concerned about time and money, so let's deal with them head on. My fee for this assignment is £5,000, which I understand is a lot of money. My proposed approach will create far more value for you. We estimated together it could create a financial benefit of £50,000, which increases your investment tenfold. That sounds like a pretty good deal, right?"

Client: "Yes, we did calculate that value together, tenfold is a good outcome."

You: "You wouldn't get that from keeping your money in a bank."

Client: "No, you wouldn't."

You: "Ok. Let's explore your second primary concern, which is your time. How many hours do you currently work?"

Client: "Oh, I guess 70 hours on a good week, more likely closer to 80 hours on a normal week, if there is such a thing."

You: "Is that sustainable? Would you agree that if you don't change something soon, you're going to continue pushing yourself towards burning out?"

Client: "Up until now, I've felt pretty strong, but more recently, I've felt a bit jaded. My wife and I have recently agreed that I can't keep this pace up for much longer."

You: "I thought so. I reckon that our work will consume around six hours a week, let's say one hour per day. That's your time investment. But it's just like your financial investment—

there'll be a large payback. There's never a good time to start this kind of work, but it sounds like it will be worth putting in a small additional effort over the short term to get a whole lot of time back. What would you do with all that extra time?"

Client: "I would like to say that I'd spend more time with my family. But, if I'm honest with myself, I'd split it 50/50 between work and family."

You: "Let's summarise. You can decide not to progress and continue working so hard for the same money. Or you can spend a little time and money with me to improve your current position tenfold. Which option would you like to go for?"

The Stephen Fry Close

The Stephen Fry close is a variation on the Boris Johnson close. It uses the same approach of using a list of pros and cons, but in this version you write them down in front of the client. They'll find it both useful and honest that you're helping them work through the positives and negatives like this. Here's an example discussion:

You: "Rather than making the decision on a gut feeling, can I suggest that we use a method that Stephen Fry uses to make a difficult decision? He's recognised as being a clever chap. He uses a straightforward method to solve complex problems: he takes a sheet of paper and draws a line down the middle. On one side, he writes the reasons against one course of action and on the other side, he lists the reasons why he should take a course of action. That way, he has everything down on one sheet of paper that allows him to make his decision. Does that sound logical?"

Client: "Sure, that seems straightforward."

You: "Good. Let's work through your thoughts and list the reasons why you should or shouldn't go ahead with our project."

Then you do just that. Take a piece of A4 paper or even a flip chart if you want to go big. Draw a line down the middle and on one side write the heading 'cons' and then 'pros' on the other side. Then you tell them:

You: "There are lots of reasons to buy the service today. Number one, you like the solution."

Write that down, but don't write the number for each point as this will make the client try to identify as many cons as pros. Write 'you like it' as the first point in the pro's column because clients often buy what they want, not what they need. Then ask for number two on the list, but remember not to write the number.

You: "You feel this option will provide a healthy return on your financial outlay".

Write that down, and then continue to extract as many reasons as possible why they should buy today. Then move onto the cons list:

You: "Ok, now for the cons. The main reason you might not sign up today is...."

At this point, write down the top three concerns they raised when you were talking through your proposal. You need to initiate this and write down the main concerns they've given you during the meeting. If you don't do it first, they will, and you'll lose control of the conversation.

Then say nothing, even if there is an awkward silence. Let the client break the silence and allow them to list any more reasons they have for not buying your service. If you've established your credibility and talked through the benefits, they won't be able to think of many and there will be many more pros than cons. Now add up the number for each column.

You: "So that's ten reasons why you should buy today and

four reasons you shouldn't."

Write the numbers at the bottom of each column big and bold. Then hand the piece of paper to the client and ask them which of those columns carries the most weight. Say nothing and let them come to their own conclusion.

Client: "Looking at this, it's pretty clear that we should start the work, it looks like the logical thing to do."

You: "That's great, should we start next Monday?"

The Assumption Close

The assumption close is one of the most natural approaches to closing the sale. It does, however, require some confidence to pull off. It's when you talk past the sale as if they have already agreed to the work and purchased your services. You don't bother asking them for a decision on whether they're going to buy your service, but talk about how much benefit they will gain now that they've agreed. Tell them how confident you are that they will attain value from the assignment.

As an example, you might say, "You're going to get some wonderful benefits from this project very quickly. When you sign up, we'll confirm your order within one hour and start within two days. No other firm can mobilise their team so soon."

The client will be able to visualise being involved in the project and enjoying the benefits of the work. They'll also gain a sense of how well organised you are.

You could then continue: "We'll start at 9 am sharp. I'll bring the coffee—do you prefer latte or cappuccino? We'll start by hanging large sheets of brown paper on the wall and we'll draw all over them to map the critical processes."

Whatever you decide to say, your aim is to talk past the sale and paint exciting and emotional pictures of the client enjoying the outcomes of your work and all the benefits that flow from it. The more vivid you paint the mental images, the more persuasive your proposal becomes.

The Escalation Close

While the assumption close is one of the easiest to use, the escalation close is one of the most effective. Although the client will be aware of what you're doing, most of them will go along with it and smile.

The escalation close involves asking a series of questions, each one leading to the next. The questions are crafted so that the obvious answer to them is "yes." You'll need to plan the questions before the meeting to make sure you get it right on the day.

One of the best ways to plan is to start with the end in mind. So, what's your end question? It's to ask for the business. Now work backwards to identify positive questions that are easy for the client to say "yes" to. Think through how one question will flow from one to another.

The first question you ask is just as important as the last, so plan your approach to asking the first question to ensure a "yes". This will then create momentum for the following positive answers. Articulate the reasons why the client should say "yes" to your first question. Then ask the following questions that also require a "yes", right up until the final question asking for the business:

You: "Hi, it's a beautiful morning, isn't it?"

Client: "Yes, it really is quite nice."

You: "May I take a seat?"

Client: "Yes, of course."

You: "I'd like to start by talking you through the proposal, is that ok?"

Client: "Yes"

You: "My understanding is that company XYZ is your competitor. Is that correct?"

Client: "Yes"

You: "…and they've been growing because they offer a similar product at a lower price. In fact, aren't they about half the price?"

Client: "Yes, it is rather annoying, we can't figure out how they're doing it."

You: "…and you'd like to reduce the cost of your product, right?"

Client: "Yes"

You: "Would I be right in saying that your thoughts are that a reduction in cost will help you regain market share?"

Client: "Yes, we're pretty confident a lot of the market will come back to us."

You: "So, if you found an approach and expertise that can drastically reduce your costs, you'd want to start right away, wouldn't you?"

Client: "Yes, you bet I would."

You: "So what do you say, shall we go for it and start the work on Monday?"

Client: "Yes, let's do it!"

The questions started out with a general question that was easy for them to say "yes" to. Then each proceeding question became more specific but provided an easy opportunity for the client to say "yes".

The escalation close uses a well-established and proven technique to get people to agree with you. It's based on the compelling psychology of repetitive affirmative answers. When you ask a client six or more questions which require them to say "yes", the client will tend to nod their head and agree with almost everything you say. In other words, once you have the client saying "yes", it becomes difficult for them to say "no."

If you try to ask all these questions in quick succession, what you're doing will be obvious and the client might take offence. So, weave them into the general conversation at the start of the meeting, then pepper them throughout your presentation until you want the client to agree to your proposal. If done well, the client will become aware of what you're doing and almost laugh at themselves each time they say "yes". They'll know what you're doing but enjoy the skilful way you're doing it, and they'll enjoy the journey.

The Triple Question Close

This closing method is a similar but shorter version of the escalation close. It is simple and effective and is used near the end of the sales meeting when you're confident that the client is convinced your service will be beneficial. As the name suggests, the close consists of three structured questions. Here's an example of the three questions a management consultant could use:

"Can you see how this would increase the productivity of your staff?"

"Are you interested in increasing the staff's productivity?"

"If you were to raise productivity when would be the best time to start?"

The three questions can be adapted for all consultants and coaches, regardless of their specialism. Here's an example of how a life coach could use the triple question close:

"Can you see how this would make you more decisive and reduce the time it takes to make important decisions?"

"Are you interested in eliminating the procrastination you suffer from?"

"If you were going to begin being more decisive when would be the best time to start?"

The first question is set so the client confirms they understand that you can help them. The second paints the picture of them addressing their challenge or achieving their ambition. The last question always aims to tie the client down to deciding to hire you. If you've built credibility and trust with them, more often than not this close will win you the work.

The Quaternary Close

Sometimes, just when you are getting into your stride and you think everything is going well, the sales conversation can come to a shuddering halt with the dreaded "Let me think about it" response.

When this happens, try not to let your disappointment show. Here's an example of how to close in this scenario:

You: "That's fine, I'm glad you want to think about it. That means you're interested in it and we are having a serious conversation. Am I right in thinking you are interested?"

Client: "Yes, yes, I'm very interested, I just want to think it through before making my decision."

You: "Ok, I guess that's to reduce the possibility of making the wrong choice. Is that correct?"

Client: "Precisely, I want to make sure I'm making the right decision before committing."

You: "I get it. It is not so much that the length of time is important to you. If I understand you, your main objective is to be as sure as possible that you are making the right decision. It doesn't matter if you need two minutes or two days, it's making the right decision that's the important thing. Isn't that right?"

Client: "Yes, I need to consider all the facts before making the decision."

You: "Great, let's double check you have everything you need to allow you to come to the right decision, which is what you want, isn't it?"

Client: "I think I have all the information I need, but I'm happy to do that."

You: "When it comes to this kind of decision, there are four questions you need to satisfy yourself with. You've already answered positively to the first three.

Do you like it?
Do you want it?
Can you afford it?

So, there's one remaining question, which is when do you want to start enjoying the benefits? You're the only person who can answer that. Let me ask you a question. The price will remain the same in the short term and in all likelihood increase in the longer term. You attain the benefits once you confirm you want the assignment to start. So, it comes down to when you want to start enjoying the benefits that will come from our work, doesn't it?

You like the proposal and how I work with clients, and you want it and can afford it. Doesn't it make sense to take the decisive step to cross the line now to attain the benefits?"

Client: "Mmm, I do need the benefits sooner rather than later. Ok, let's take that step and start the work."

There are four clear questions used in this close. However, before you ask them, the client needs to agree that the reason they say they want to think about it is not down to needing more time. Once you remove the 'time' objection, you can move the discussion on to the 'information' elements.

All you need to do is to presume that they like it, want it and can afford it, and get them to confirm this. After that, the only possible question left is based on when the client wishes to attain the benefits.

The Trivial Close

The first few times you use a pre-planned close it can feel a little unnatural. If you think you might feel this way, then the trivial close might be a good option for you.

It's a straightforward approach that involves an unimportant element of your proposal. If a client agrees to that small element, they've indicated that they have made their mind up to hire you.

For example, if a client shows interest in working with you, use a trivial question, such as, "Would you prefer the final report in PowerPoint or in Word?" The format of the report is a minor point; buying your service is the primary issue. If the client says their preference is for PowerPoint, for example, they have, by extension, made up their mind to purchase your offer and start the assignment. Here are a few examples of how this can work:

"What dress code would you like us to adopt?"

"Would you like to hold the review meetings in person or by video conference?"

"Would you prefer us to use our logo or yours on the presentations to the board?"

All of these are trivial points, but they help the client through that uncomfortable point in the sales process—the moment of indecision that is part and parcel of making a substantial commitment, both financial and emotional. Getting the client to concentrate on a trivial point makes it easy for them to say "yes" to the small stuff and eases them into saying "yes" to the big stuff.

The Deal or No Deal Close

This form of closure is one of my favourites, and I use it most frequently and most successfully. It's not manipulative or cheesy, but it does help both you and the client get the most value from the sales conversation.

This close is used right at the start of the meeting, not at the end. If allowed, a large proportion of clients will say something like, "Thanks for talking me through your proposal, I would like some time to think about it". A variation of the client's comment could also be, "Ok, that's great, I love it, I need to talk it over with my boss." We all know nine times out of ten it will end up with you chasing them for an answer and creating tension for both of you. The result will be the client returning your call a few weeks later to turn you down. Worst of all, the relationship will be damaged because you had to push hard to get an answer.

To avoid this all too common but avoidable scenario, tell them you're going to ask them to make a decision. Make the request right at the start of the meeting, and then ask the 'deal or no deal' question at the end of your presentation. Here's an example:

You: "Hi, thanks for meeting me today."

Client: "That's fine, we've been talking for a while, I'm keen to listen to your ideas."

You: "Good to hear. We've had an interesting discussion over four weeks now, and I think I've given you enough information to get a good understanding of what I do and how we'd work together."

Client: "Yes, I like everything I've heard, that's why we're still talking."

You: "I've also sent you a proposal about how best to achieve your ambitions, which I'll talk you through today, and I'll answer any remaining questions you might have. By the end of this meeting, you'll have all the information you need to make a decision one way or another. So, I will be asking you to tell me today if you'd like to proceed or not. Is that ok?"

Client: "Ok, that makes sense. I've read your proposal and have a pretty good grasp of your offer."

You then take the client through your proposal. Use the sandwich close described in the previous step to tell them the price. Then ask for the work.

Client: "I like your proposal, and it sits well with me. I think I'm going to go for it, but let me chew it over, and I'll come back to you to with an answer."

You: "I appreciate that, but you have all the information you need to make the decision today. You did agree at the start of our meeting that you'd decide if you're going to proceed today."

There will be a little bit of silence at this point, and the client will have a wry smile on their face as they acknowledge to themselves that they did commit to making the decision. Let them have one or two seconds then come back in before they respond.

You: "After what you said about the challenges you face and where you'd like to take the company, it seems this is the perfect time to start. Unless there is something that I haven't explained. Don't you think we should start sooner rather than later?"

This puts the client into a position where they need to provide a reason for their hesitation or objection. In either case, this will surface any remaining concerns, which you can then address and continue to ask for the work.

If after all this, the client still asks for more time to consider your proposal, there is nothing you can do. You cannot continue the sales conversation unless you have an objection you can respond to. Using the deal or no deal close from the outset of the meeting will give the client three potential routes:

Deal
No deal
I need more information to decide

The option of delaying the decision is removed, as the client agreed to make a choice at the meeting. The client could still say "no", but at least you will know and will act accordingly. To summarise: at the start of the meeting, tell them that you will ask for a definite answer and get them to agree to that. Then when the time is right, ask for them to make the decision. If they try to delay, remind them that they committed to giving you an answer and ask if there's any more information they require. Deal with their objections and ask for the business again. Rinse and repeat until you get a solid "yes" or "no".

The Pocket Close

This approach works well for coaches and for consultants who work with clients on a one-to-one basis. Whether you are a coach or a consultant, this close works best when the assignment is to work with a client on something personal or emotional.

The close kicks in when you, the coach, have finished talking the client through how you work with people and the benefits they experience but the client has resistance to signing up because of financial concerns. It's a powerful way to demonstrate that they should not focus on finances, but the original reason they came to you. If a client starts to umm and ahh because of money, do this:

You: "I can see the financial aspect weighs heavily with you."

Client: "Yes, I don't have a lot of spare cash at the moment. I know I could do with your help, but I'm just not sure I can afford it."

You: "Would you mind standing up for a moment, please, I'd like to demonstrate something to you."

Both of you stand, and you hand the client a small glass marble, the kind you used to play with as a child.

You: "Please, can you take this marble and put it in your pocket. Good. I'd like to ask you to walk around the room for a little. I want you to think about how it feels. The marble feels small and light, right? I bet after a few hours you would forget it was even there. What do you think?"

Client: "Yes, it's not uncomfortable. I would soon get used to it."

You: "Ok, I would like you to do the same but this time with this squash ball. Put it in your pocket and walk around with it, then tell me how it feels."

Client: "Right, I can feel it, I'm aware of it, and it's a bit annoying, but it is not too bothersome."

You: "Let's take it a step further. Here's a cricket ball. You'd struggle to get it to fit in your pocket, wouldn't you? You might be able to squeeze it in, but it would be uncomfortable. You could hold it everywhere you go and grasp it during every movement you make, but not only would you be aware of it, it would be at the forefront of your mind. Imagine if you had to carry it around for weeks."

Client: "Ok, I get it. Yes, if I were to carry the cricket ball around all day, I wouldn't forget it like the marble, and it would start to annoy me after a few days."

You: "I'm sure you know where I'm going with this. Consider carrying the cricket ball around for months, or even years. It would feel like you were carrying a bowling ball. You could do it, but not for long.

If you wait too long, the issue, the reason you came to me, will feel like carrying a bowling ball. You just won't be able to do it, and you'll end up dropping it exhausted and with no strength left."

There will be a few seconds, where the client stares into your eyes or looks at their feet as they digest what you've demonstrated.

You: "Do you want to carry the marble, the squash ball, the cricket ball, or the bowling ball?"

Client: "I never thought about it that way. The marble obviously, although it already feels like I'm stuck with the bowling ball."

You: "Well, let's work together to get your challenges back down to marble size, and soon enough you won't notice it's there."

Choose this close carefully. It works best when people need your help but cannot bring themselves to accept the support they need. If you try this with someone you don't know well, they won't feel comfortable enough to go with the flow. Only try this with people you've built a strong, trusting relationship with, as they'll be open enough to take on what's being said.

There is real power in creating a physical and mental jolt to produce the realisation that a client needs your help. The props you use to demonstrate the point are not important—it doesn't need to be balls. Choose your own version of this close to display what might happen if the client doesn't accept your support.

The pocket close or any variation you decide to use is compelling because it creates both an emotional epiphany and a logical reason to work with you. At this moment, the client will be more open than ever to buy your services.

The Right Brain Story Close

Your brain consists of two halves, and within each of these are particular areas that are responsible for different functions. There is a well-recognised theory that the left-hand side of the brain is responsible for logical functions such as mathematics, recalling facts, linear thinking and problem-solving, while the right-hand side is concerned with creative functions such as imagination, feelings, art and visualisation.

The same theory continues to say that people are either left- or right-brained, but not both. This means that one side of the brain is dominant. Left-brain people tend to be analytical, orderly and 'digital'. On the other hand, right-brained people are more creative and intuitive, which could be called 'analogue'.

If you think that your client is 'analogue', that is to say, the right brain is more dominant, this close might work well. This group of people react well to being told stories as they make it easy for them to visualise, feel and experience what you're telling them.

Try telling them a story about another client, similar to them, who bought your service and experienced some great results. Whenever a right-brained person hears a story about a successful client, they envisage themselves in the same situation and enjoying the same benefits.

Potential clients are often not able to recall the data and technical aspects associated with your service. After a day or two, almost all of that information will be forgotten. But they will recall the stories you told them, in some cases for months or even years. So, tell them as many relevant stories as you can muster.

You can tell them happy, positive stories about satisfied clients in similar positions to theirs. Or you can tell them sad, negative stories about people who didn't use your services and found their situation worsened. You can also tell a story about making the wrong choice, perhaps someone who decided to work with a different coach because they were less expensive.

As it turns out, you get what you pay for, and the assignment ended in disaster.

Pick the right story to create the right emotion. If a client is struggling to envisage the benefits, tell them a happy story. If they understand the potential benefits but are reticent to sign up, tell them a negative story. If you get the feeling they're going to attempt to negotiate your price down, you could weave a 'making the wrong choice' story into your conversation.

Stories work well with 'analogue', right-brained people. They can visualise and feel the emotions you invoke through your storytelling. However, don't attempt to tell a story to a 'digital', left-brained person. They'll frown and wonder why you're telling them a stupid, irrelevant story. Choose wisely, and make sure you understand your client.

※ ※ ※

Ten Steps To Win Work

Step 1—Believe in yourself
Step 2—Identify their style
Step 3—Visualise the meeting
Step 4—Plan the conversation
Step 5—Brace for objections
Step 6—Be a salesperson
Step 7—Avoid these things
Step 8—Empathise don't sympathise
Step 9—Say the price
Step 10—Close the deal

PLANNING PROGRESS

What

Plan how you are going to put everything into practice and how to monitor your performance.

Why

You're going to be busy when you start to promote your services, so it's essential to have everything in place beforehand. And, when you're running at full speed, it will be challenging to make the right decisions if you have no information to base them on.

How

Employ the plan-do-check-act structure. Plan your activities and performance, do the work, check everything is going to plan and adjust as necessary.

❋ ❋ ❋

There are two phases to getting more clients. The first is to ensure you have everything in place and a plan for how you're going to do all that preparation. The second is to put the tools, techniques and strategies you've identified into action. When you're doing this hard work to sell your services, it's vital to hold yourself accountable by using a performance tracker. I call these two phases 'develop' and 'act'.

This two-phase approach is a bit like hiring a personal fitness coach to improve your health. The first part, the 'develop' phase, would be to put your fitness plan in place. That might mean getting the right food in the fridge, resetting your alarm clock, drawing up an exercise plan, putting the exercise equipment you'll need into the garage etc. The second part, the 'act' phase, is to enact that fitness plan, do the work, get into the gym and break a sweat.

You won't get fit by drawing up a plan—the plan produces no benefit by itself. The way to get healthy (or in our case to get more clients) is to do the work, week in, week out, and track your performance monthly. There is no escape from this reality. This is where the rubber hits the road.

Step 1—Define The Goal

Imagine standing in a crowd at Wembley football stadium watching Scotland play England. One of the teams has perfect control of the ball as one player dribbles the ball past two of the opposition players. He then passes it to his teammate who crosses the ball with his first touch into the penalty box. The third player sprints with all the speed he can muster and leaps into the air to head the ball for a goal. He looks round to aim but realises something is wrong. There is no goal, no net, no goalkeeper. How can he take the shot? There is no goal to shoot at. The referee blows the whistle and confusion and chaos erupts. Players walk around the pitch lost, not knowing what direction to move in, and eventually they give up and walk off the field.

You can't play a football match without goals. The players need something to aim for in order to take a shot at hitting their target. When you don't have goals, it is all too easy to get distracted and work on something unimportant. In short order, you'll lose direction, momentum, energy and interest. You'll give up and walk off the field.

Spend some time alone with no distractions to figure out what is your end goal. This shouldn't be something that would be nice to have, but something you must have. It must be highly important to you; your future rests on it. The stronger your desire to attain this goal, the more likely you are to do the work necessary to achieve it. If it's to get more clients and increase revenue, a good goal to aim for is a 40% year-on year-uplift.

Once you've set your goal, and if it is essential, it will provide you with the power and direction to complete all your future actions. Not just any measure, but the right work that moves you closer to your goal. Each time you make a decision, ask yourself, "Will this help me achieve my goal?" If the answer is "yes" then get on and do it, but if the answer is "no" or "maybe" don't waste your time on it.

Let's say your goal is to land a client that generates assignments worth £1 million combined. Asking yourself, "Will this help me get the £1 million client?" will help you figure out if a task is a priority or not, and if it's the right thing to do.

Aim to settle on one big goal that focuses on the most crucial aspect of your professional life. This singleness of purpose acts like a light drawing you towards it. So, when you get up in the morning and start your working day, you know why you're putting in so much effort. Your thinking becomes lucid, and you'll be more relaxed and alert. You'll do what you must with a greater sense of ease, confidence and expertise.

Step 2—Set The Deadline

Someone with no real deadline to write an email to a client can spend half a day on it. They might stroll to the coffee shop, order a drink, then rummage around to find the recipient's address while being distracted by browsing Facebook. They might spend a while looking for their eyeglasses so they can see the laptop, and then realise they were on top of their head all the time. They eventually get around to composing the email, but then have to find the barista to get the Wi-Fi password.

Compare this to a focused, busy service professional who takes two minutes for the same task: one-and-a-half minutes to write the email, thirty seconds to check it, then bang—it's sent. One person ends up exhausted after spending half a day writing an important email while the other completes the task in no time with lots of energy and vim to go on to do lots of different jobs.

C. Northcote Parkinson described this phenomenon back in the 1950s. He said, "Work expands to fill time." It holds as true today as it did then and has become known as 'Parkinson's Law.'

Parkinson's Law goes on to explain that work is elastic in its demand for time. One person might take more time than another to complete the same job. But the person who takes longer is not idle or enjoying that period as leisure time. The task they perform—in this example, writing an email—grows in importance and complexity in direct correlation to the time available to complete it. If you have thirty minutes to write that email, the chances are that's how long it will take. If you only have a few minutes, it will take a few short moments to get it done. The person who took twice the time will be just as busy as the person who took half the time. That's Parkinson's Law in action: work expands to fill the time you have available.

This phenomenon causes us to both under- and overestimate how long it will take us to complete work activities. I tend to be over-optimistic on what I can achieve each day and week. I cram my schedule full of well-intentioned actions—it's a bit like London Heathrow airport that schedules its runways at 100% utilisation. If something unplanned happens, it will cause a small delay. However, the knock-on effect will amplify and accumulate, and a thirty-minute delay in the morning might end up causing a five-hour delay in the evening. And we all know that the consulting and coaching workload is variable, with lots of unforeseen tasks hurtling towards you.

While most people tend to overestimate what can be done

in a day or a week, they underestimate what can be achieved in a year. I've worked with hundreds of people to get more clients than they thought possible. I've encouraged all of them to hit two deadlines: to get everything in place to complete the 'develop' phase within three months, and to raise their revenue by 40% twelve months after that.

These goals might sound like a stretch. You might be thinking, "I'm already overburdened with work, there's no way I can do all the preparation in three months." I'd like to reassure you that if you are determined, disciplined and dedicated, you can and will achieve it. Parkinson's Law holds true for all my clients, and it applies to you, too.

Step 3—Define The Milestones

You've defined the big goal and the deadline—the 'what' and the 'when'. Now it's time to identify how you are going to do it by setting a series of milestones.

A milestone marks an important chunk of a journey. Once you reach a milestone, you know that that section is over. So when you describe each milestone for your business, it should signify you've completed a discrete phase of work. I find it helpful to start each milestone with, "When I have…". It helps to establish the significant points of progress. For example: "When I have implemented all the elements of Constructing Credibility—target date 1st December 2020." This indicates when you'll have all the physical items to hand and enough information to start quantifying your fees.

The chapters in this book serve as a good set of milestones to aim for, and I suggest you complete them in sequence. If you try to position your price before building your brand, the fees you set will be based on guesswork with no logic to support them. If you skip a milestone or work on one out of sequence, you'll be building a flawed business development system.

Chapters one to four of this book contain all the items that are required to complete the 'develop' phase. Once you've completed them, switch to the 'act' phase of promoting your services. These activities are covered in chapters five to seven. This is when you'll stay in touch with your target market, have face-to-face meetings and receive requests for proposals and new assignments.

Step 4—Plan The Activities

When working towards completing a milestone, it will help to figure out how much work lies ahead and how much time you have to complete it. Identify the things you need to do to achieve each milestone. As before, use this book to define each action and complete them in the sequence suggested.

Step 5—Identify The Dependencies

Are there activities on your list that you can't do yourself and need some help with? Review your 'develop' plan and identify where you don't have the expertise or inclination to complete specific tasks. Most people find they need support creating some of the outputs described in chapter two, Constructing Credibility, so don't be afraid to hire someone to create business cards, build a better website, get some professional photographs or even proofread and improve your articles.

If you are going to hire outside help, make sure you book their services well in advance. Tell them when you want them to complete the work you assign to them. We all need a little help. The trick is to be honest with yourself, recognise the help you need and then do something about it. The experts I use to help my business grow and develop are:

Writing coach—to become a better author

Personal coach—to help deal with the ups and downs of life

Graphic designer—to design my logo and colour schemes

Commercial lawyer—to draft robust and fair terms and conditions for business contracts

If you think you'd benefit from getting support in one of these disciplines let me know, and I'd be happy to introduce you to the people I rely on. My contact details are at the end of the book.

Step 6—Manage The Risks

Now you've set the goals, deadlines, milestones, activities and their dependencies, it's time to think the unthinkable. What could go wrong? Most plans don't pan out the way you expect, some will go wrong or be completed later than hoped. In the words of the former US Secretary of State Donald Rumsfeld:

> "As we know, there are known knowns; there are things we know we know. We also know there are known unknowns; that is to say, we know there are some things we do not know. But there are also unknown unknowns, the ones we don't know we don't know... It is the latter category that tends to be the difficult ones."

This can make things tricky when it comes to identifying risks. It's impossible to deal with the 'unknown unknowns' beforehand, so try not to stress about them too much—nobody knows what's around the corner. It's crucial to adopt a pragmatic approach to risk management. It's all too easy to go down the rabbit hole and get lost in the hundreds of things that could go wrong.

Try this. Take a sheet of paper and write along the top: 'Things that could go wrong, and if they do, it will cause a problem'. Now write a list of the main risks that come to mind for the implementation phase. If you're anything like me, you'll come up with a lot. In fact, when I did this exercise, the list extended to over 100 items. If you sit down and think through all the milestones and activities, a lot could go wrong, and long delays could be incurred.

But if you try to manage all the risks, you'll end up focusing so hard on making sure the bad stuff doesn't happen that you'll have no time for the positive things. You can't deal with all the potential risks before they arise.

The best way to focus your energy is to prioritise the potential issues by considering two factors: severity and likelihood. If a potential problem would only have a small impact on your timeline and there is little chance of it happening, don't worry about. However, if there's a risk that would cause a severe delay, you should do something about it before it becomes a problem.

My general rule of thumb is that low and medium risks should have contingency plans ready to deploy if something goes wrong. High and critical risks are a different matter. If you recognise a risk that falls into one of these categories, you must do something to mitigate it straight away so you can fix it before it happens.

Step 7—Implement Management Systems

You'll find it useful to monitor performance when you're getting everything ready during the 'develop' phase, and also for the recurring sales tasks you'll use in the 'act' period.

The best performance management systems originate from Japanese automotive manufactures. Companies such as Toyota, Nissan and Honda have exceptional efficiency and effectiveness, both in project management and manufacturing. The approach I use, and which is described in this chapter, is a planning and monitoring process based on the concept these companies use called Hoshin Kanri.

Hoshin Kanri was born from Japanese manufacturers' seven tools of quality control, and these are based on the seven martial arts weapons described in 'A Book of Five Rings', an ancient guide for Benkei samurai warrior monks. *Ho* means 'method' or 'form' and *shin* means 'shiny needle' or 'compass'—in other words, 'direction'. *Kanri* means 'movement' or 'action'. Overall, it's a method of integrating daily activities with long-term goals.

In essence, the term is aiming to convey that you're heading for a destination with the compass pointing you in the right direction, and you have broken down the overall journey into a step-by-step plan to get you there. The best way to obtain your desired goals is to ensure that you understand and commit to your long-term direction and work according to a detailed plan to make your vision a reality. The second aspect is that there are fundamental process measures which must be monitored to ensure your goals are achieved.

The method is hierarchical. You start by defining the goals of the project, setting deadlines, defining critical milestones, identifying the activities and understanding the dependencies and risks. The next step is to put in place a management system to track your performance.

Develop Phase: Project Plan

I find the best way to plan and monitor progress during the 'develop' phase is by using a simplified Gantt chart. This method is named after Henry Gantt, who designed the approach in the early 1900s. The first Gantt charts were drawn on paper but, as you would expect, today there are many project management software packages and mobile phone apps that use Gantt charts. My advice is not to bother with these, as they are too complex for what you need. A simple spreadsheet will do the job.

On the chart, actions are shown on the vertical axis while the scheduled time spent is laid out on the horizontal axis. Each task is represented by a bar that shows the time required for the project. It's straightforward to create one for your project:

List all the milestones and activities in sequence down the left-hand side.

Draw a horizontal axis that represents the three-month implementation period and divide it into 12 weekly columns.

Draw horizontal bars in line with each activity to show when each one is to start and finish.

Update the chart to review progress and decide if any solutions are needed to get the project back on track.

There are lots of examples and templates on the internet, if your Google 'Gantt chart', you'll be spoiled for choice.

Act Phase: Performance Tracker

The adage 'What gets measured, gets managed' is true when it comes to selling consulting and coaching services. An effective sales manager will have a rock solid business-building system in place and a means to monitor and manage three aspects of their sales activity. The key aspects of monitoring are:

Watch indicators: are you doing enough background work to generate face-to-face meetings?

Driver numbers: are you focusing on business development activities?

Financial results: are you creating enough business?

Here are some metrics and targets you will find it useful:

Watch indicators performance:

Watch Indicators	Description	Target
Invite people to an event	Number of people registering for your event	20 / month
Promotion Materials	Number of articles, brochures, or videos produced	2 / month
LinkedIn	Number of articles, videos, or offers posted	2 / month
Writing	Number of words written to be used in articles or for your book	2000 / month
Events	Number of events presenting your knowledge and services	1 / month

Driver numbers performance:

Driver Numbers	Description	Target
Group of 80	Number of people contacted	80 / month
Roll of 20	Number of people contacted	20 / month
Clique of 10	Number of referrals received or given	10 / month
Individual Enquiries	Number of enquiries/phone calls received	4 / month
Relationship meetings	Number of face-to-face meetings	2 / month

Financial results performance:

Financial Results	Description	Target
Service 1	Revenue	Set a monthly target based on the big goal
Service 2	Revenue	Set a monthly target based on the big goal
Service 3	Revenue	Set a monthly target based on the big goal

If you'd like a copy of the implementation Gantt chart templates or the operational performance tracker template I use, send me an email with your contact details. Ask for the template and let me know what you think of the book, and I'll post a blank copy of the document in the format my clients and I use. My email address is peter@byscoachinggroup.com

Step 8—Take Decisive Action

You have everything in place and the means to monitor progress. Now it's time to do the work. If we go back to the fitness coach analogy, it's time to hit the gym. Remember: success comes from taking consistent, decisive action.

The life coach Tony Robbins has a lot to say on this subject, and I agree with him. It's your commitment to doing the work necessary to get more clients that will determine your level of success.

There's a vast gulf between being *committed* to achieving your goals and being *interested* in them. You're fooling yourself if you say, "I would like to increase my revenue" or "It would be nice to be recognised as an expert in my field." These are gentle statements; they don't represent decisive commitments. It's a bit like saying "I'm interested in achieving my goals, as long as it doesn't involve hard work." What decisions do you need to make to commit to achieving your big goal?

If you've made the decision to commit, now it's time to act. It is easy to start missing targets if you don't have a recurring daily schedule. You'll end up putting something off till the next day, and these activities will roll over to double the workload, accumulating each day until you have too much to do. Left unchecked, it will become harder and harder to catch up to get back to where you should be.

Once your actions start to slip, so will your attitude, which will in turn affect your activities more. You'll be locked into a destructive cycle which is increasingly hard to break free from. If you are to achieve success, you must commit to making positive decisions daily that move you ever closer to your goal.

To avoid the downward spiral, take the monthly targets in the performance tracker and break down the metrics into a standard daily routine. There are roughly 20 working days each month, so:

2000 words written a month = 100 per day

Reaching out to 20 people = one person per day

£10,000 revenue a month = £500 per day

Don't try to 'eat the elephant' in one go. Break it down into smaller, more manageable chunks.

Step 9—Check On Progress

In the early 1600s, Francis Bacon established what is now known as the 'scientific method'. Later, in the mid-1900s, W. Edward Deming used the scientific method to create an approach called the 'plan-do-check-act' (PDCA) cycle. Since then, most modern-day performance management systems have used PDCA as their backbone.

The work you do in both the 'develop' and 'act' phases follow the same PDCA cycle.

Plan—who, what, where, when, why, how

Do—complete the planned activities

Check—are the activities and performance going to plan?

Act—if something is going wrong

Aim to check the status monthly and, once you settle into a steady rhythm, monitor the ongoing recurring work. More frequently would lead to you spending more time checking than doing, but less often and you run the risk of leaving it too late to recognise something is wrong.

Step 10—Deal With Problems

We've already established that not everything will go right the first time and that you should use the management systems to spot when things aren't going to plan. So, what should you do when a problem arises? The problem with problem-solving is that you'll already have solved all the easy ones. It's the hidden ones that come flying around the corner and smack you in the face that causes the most significant difficulties, the 'unknown unknowns'.

If you're going to fix a problem, you need to first examine it. Understand what's really going on rather than assuming you already know what's gone wrong. A problem well defined is a problem half-solved.

> *I keep six honest serving-men*
> *They taught me all I knew*
> *Their names are What and Why and*
> *When and Where And Who.*
>
> RUDYARD KIPLING

Take Rudyard Kipling's advice and, when faced with a problem, ask What? Why? When? Where? and Who? to gain better insight into the situation. Once you know the answers, implement a solution to ensure you still achieve your project plan or performance target.

❋ ❋ ❋

Ten Steps To Plan Progress

Step 1—Define the goal
Step 2—Set the deadline
Step 3—Define the milestones
Step 4—Plan the activities
Step 5—Identify the dependencies
Step 6—Manage the risks
Step 7—Implement management systems
Step 8—Take decisive action
Step 9—Check on progress
Step 10—Deal with problems

PERSONAL POWER

What

Personal power creates momentum and is the defining factor of the success of your business. It's not a set of techniques or steps to follow, but a collection of positive principles that can help create a strong foundation to reach your goals.

Why

We all allow ourselves to adopt beliefs and principles that are limiting, disempowering and destructive. If left to take root and grow, they can strangle your motivation, energy and confidence. You'll achieve a small fraction of what you are capable of, and that includes winning more clients.

How

There are certain principles that will help you create your own personal power. Some of them might resonate with you, and some might not. Being yourself means that you should explore this chapter with an open mind to find and use your own personal power principles.

※ ※ ※

We all dream about making our business a rip-roaring success and building a reputation as the 'go-to' person when a client needs help. We also dream about coupling a satisfying and rewarding career with a blissful personal life.

In both of these areas, being yourself is key. And a critical element that will help you achieve your dreams is the principle of personal power. Only you can make things happen. Only you can make yourself feel how you feel. And only you can make your business a success. You, my friend, are in control of your destiny.

In everyday life we all use only a small percentage of our abilities, energy and brainpower. You'd be surprised just how much is left on the table.

Do you know what you are capable of? Most people don't realise their true potential and self-restrict what they do to stay within their comfort zone. The famous ultra-athlete David Goggins achieves some astounding feats of strength and endurance. He runs and wins 100-mile races and has performed more than 4,000 continuous pull-ups in 17 hours. He might be super fit and strong, but do you think that's what gets him from the 99th mile to the hundredth, or from the 4,029th pull-up to the 4,030th?

No. It's his personal power—the principles unique to him—that lie behind his extraordinary achievements. He believes that most people live at about 40% of their capability. He says:

> *From the time you take your first breath, you become eligible to die. You also become eligible to find your greatness. But it is up to you to equip yourself for the battle ahead. Only you can master your mind, which is what it takes to live a bold life filled with accomplishments most people consider beyond their capability.*

Throughout this book, I've offered a practical step-by-step guide on how to get more clients. I can't offer you the same guidance when it comes to identifying and utilising your unique personal powers, or, in the next chapter, how to appreciate your adventure. What I can do is to present some helpful principles. They are did not originate from me, but I've adopted and adapted them to suit my requirements. I've researched and studied many successful people: world-class business leaders, athletes, actors and thought leaders. These are the principles that work for me, and I think they will also work for you. However, it's important to find your own. Listen to others, do some research, then make your own mind up based on your personal principles. Be yourself.

Step 1—Use Empowering Words

Why is it that three people can go through the same event but have different experiences and emotions? For example, think of a long line of people queuing for a ride on a roller coaster. Let's say in that queue are four teenagers, waiting their turn for the ride. One might be bored, the other excited, the third might be lost in thought about where they will eat that evening, and the fourth could be angry at the long wait. Four people all in the same situation, yet four different experiences. Why?

There is a beautiful book by Eckhart Tolle called *The Power of Now*. In it he uses the enlightening phrase, 'Wherever you go, there you are'. If you're an angry person, no matter where you go, you'll find things that annoy you. However, if you are a happy and jovial, the word will be a different place.

It might not be obvious, but a lot of what we feel is down to the words we use. How we speak has a significant influence on the way we perceive, think and react to the world around us. This, in turn, shapes the paradigms we work in. We select words that over time become habitual. Words are powerful; they can transform our life experiences. In fact, the words we use to describe our experience will become our experience.

Few people appreciate how much the words they use, correlate with the personal power they exude. Words affect how they talk to themselves and, therefore, what they experience. Using emotional and passionate words can change what you think and feel. If you use disempowering, negative words, they will bring you down. So, stop and make the conscious decision to replace them with empowering, positive ones.

What if you could take all your negative emotions, thoughts and feelings and be able to toss them over your shoulder, never to experience them again. Sounds good, right? Choosing positive, power-building words will dampen down negative emotions and smash your positive ones through the roof.

The words we use can be a product of where we have lived or live. I'm from Scotland, and we have many names for calling someone stupid: *Glaikit, heid-the-baw, bampot, dunce, diddy, fandan, radge, walloper, daftie, eejit, tube...* the list goes on. But guess what? I took these words on and internalised them. It took me quite some time after leaving Scotland not to feel stupid. The words I used had brought my personal power to rock-bottom. Scotland is a great place, and the Scottish people are the best in the world. However, I'm convinced that their trait of never quite achieving what they're capable of is in part down to their lexicon.

Choose ten negative words that you frequently use and write them down as a list. Now choose ten new words to replace them that are more positive. Here are ten words I used to say to myself and others, and what I chose to say instead:

Depressed = mellow
Tired = a little jaded
Hurt = twinge
Angry = miffed
Disrespectful = cheeky
Stupid = discovering
Overwhelmed = in demand
Stressed = busy
Frustrated = fascinated
Furious = passionate

Using softer words will soften their effect on you. What were your words, and what have you decided to change them to?

Here's something you might not be comfortable with but you'll get a great benefit from. Post your list of negative and replacement words somewhere prominent in your house or office. Tell your family, friends and close colleagues about your banned words. Ask them to remind you of your replacement word whenever you slip into using a negative phrase. Make a conscious effort to practise and you'll start to dampen down your power-sapping emotions.

Now, repeat the process, but this time take a different perspective by thinking about the words you use to describe positive situations and experiences. List ten positive, power-building words that you use. Now it's time to identify replacement words that slingshot your personal power into a different league to get an even greater benefit from them. Here are the words I now use to boost my outlook on life:

Fine = awesome
Good = incredible
Great = phenomenal
Alright = Superb
Not bad = tremendous
Okay = wonderful
Happy = ecstatic
Nice = fantastic
Perfect = extraordinary
Satisfied = out of this world

As with your other list, post these somewhere visible and make a concerted effort to drop your power-limiting words and replace them with alternatives. Use these words to drive your personal power to new heights.

Step 2—Pursue Balanced Wellbeing

I'm not a doctor, nutritionist or fitness coach. Everything I tell you about wellbeing is what works for me; you will need to research and seek professional advice to figure out what works for you.

For me, there are two main aspects of wellbeing that boost power: physical and mental health, and how you present yourself to your clients. Physical and mental wellness can improve how you view yourself and it will help you make the best first impression with your new client, too. Let's not forget: you make first impressions quickly, but they're slowly forgotten.

I used to work lots of hours as a management consultant—an unhealthy amount. I would start the day at 4 am to manage the teams in Asia, then work through the day with the European teams. I would then work through to around 10 pm to manage our teams in America. I was working 18 hours a day, getting by on four or five hours of sleep, eating convenience processed food, and not finding the time or energy to exercise.

One morning I dragged myself out of bed at 3:30 am and stumbled into the bathroom. I looked in the mirror and didn't recognise the person staring back at me. I saw an old grey man. I was 45, but I looked 65. The person in front of me had grey hair, grey skin, grey teeth and grey stubble. I looked down at his grey t-shirt and saw a sizeable swollen barrel of a belly sticking out. I noticed the bags under his eyes and looked closer to see that there were bags under the bags.

Who was this person? It couldn't be me, could it? It was. I looked old, tired and unhealthy. Who would want to hire this old, unenergised shadow of my former self? I wasn't exactly the energetic, smart professional clients would queue up to work with.

I knew that on the days I worked from home my hygiene was less of a priority than the pressing work issues of the day. I could gain an extra ten minutes if I skipped the shower, another five if I didn't shave. After working from home for three or four days on the trot, my self-respect would hit rock bottom. Gone was the vibrant expert in productivity, and in his place was a slow-thinking has-been. My motivation, energy, enthusiasm and confidence had been chipped away. And a telling sign of my downhill slide was that my sales performance had flat-lined. The flow of new work I used to generate was dead.

In a perfect world, your appearance shouldn't influence your ability to sell. But in reality, looks matter. There have been many studies on this topic, and they all show that attractive people generate higher sales. It might not be politically correct but, like it or not, buyers judge. Your appearance matters—to your own self-worth, to your clients, and to your sales performance. Clients might like to think their decision to hire a consultant or coach is made on an objective basis, but subconsciously they are judging how you present yourself. And you are also judging yourself, which affects your confidence and happiness. And let's not forget: happy people sell.

I was a mess. I knew that, if I were a client, I would not hire me. So, I decided to make a conscious effort to turn things around. Don't get me wrong, I'm not a super fit, attractive model on the front cover of GQ magazine. However, I now make every effort to make the best of what I've got. This keeps me sharp, energetic, confident and most of all, happy. On top of this, I now have the head space to hear what my clients are saying.

I adopted five powerful practices to improve my health and ramp up my personal power:

Getting up early
Getting some exercise
Getting good clothes
Getting nutritious food
Getting quality sleep

Think of the first four of these practices as the four legs of a table, creating a solid foundation. Getting up early, exercising, putting on good clothes and eating well are the four legs which need a steady tabletop of plenty of quality sleep.

Step 3—Get up early

Get up before the sun. You might not want to hear this, and I thought long and hard about including this subject in the book, but it's my firm belief that to sell your services and grow your business, you should get up early in the morning.

Getting up early might sound like a fashionable thing to say and something celebrities proclaim to do. And it's not essential to get up early to get that long line of clients queueing to work with you. But it sure helps. How can you ever make the day your own if you can't carve out some time in the morning to make yourself achieve your full potential? You can try to protect two power hours later in the morning, but it's pretty hard when everyone else is up demanding your time.

How you start your day will have a considerable influence on your productivity and the value you generate. In today's environment, if you allow them, distractions and conflicting priorities will suck you into being overburdened and inefficient. You'll kick your legs just to tread water and keep yourself from drowning in the deluge of unimportant 'stuff'.

Getting up early to take charge of the day is a difficult discipline to master. But with a little determination and effort, it can be done. Scientists and performance coaches call this a 'keystone habit'. Make no mistake, it can be tough to make getting up early a habit, an automatic action. There will be days when you want to stay in bed and need a lunchtime power nap. But, if you stick at it, you'll soon make it part of your day. Your body and brain will adjust, reset, and even thrive from the practice.

What is your current morning routine? Perhaps you get up at 7 am, rush around to get the kids ready for school, get yourself dressed for work, then skip breakfast to jump in the car. If you got up early, there would be no more rushing into the day unprepared. You would banish the craziness and take control of your day.

Perhaps you're thinking, "Yes, I get it, but let's get serious and come back to real life. I'm already stressed because I have too much on my shoulders. My schedule has back-to-back meetings, and in some cases, I'm double-booked, and that's only my work commitments. My family and friends also need my time. There's no way I can squeeze more into my day."

I understand. But less is more. You're attempting to fit too much into your day, and it's better to complete one masterpiece than a hundred average works of art. Remember: you are trying to establish yourself as one of the leading experts in your field so you can charge high fees and work fewer hours. Clients won't consider you an expert if your work is average. In the world of coaching and consulting, less is more.

Take two hours in the morning for yourself. Take control of the day before somebody else does it for you. However, don't squander this time drinking coffee and watching breakfast television. It's not just getting up early that makes the difference.

Step 4—Get Some Exercise

Start the day by throwing a strong coffee down your throat and get exercising. Do it before your brain kicks in and comes up with a bunch of reasons why you don't have time. That's the first of the two extra hours used. After that, spend thirty minutes eating a healthy breakfast and thirty minutes planning what you're going to achieve that day. If you do these three things before most people get out of bed, you'll put yourself in the best possible position to seize the day.

Maybe you're not a morning person. That's fine. The important thing is that you carve out two hours of the day to perform focused, uninterrupted work. Whenever is your time, find a moment when life is calm and straightforward, when the world is peaceful and there is little to disturb or interrupt. For many busy service professionals, the morning is the only point in the day they have to themselves to concentrate on their priorities. Carving out that time is a symbol of the control you have over life. It allows you to focus on your goals and as a result, can be empowering.

There are so many benefits from exercise that it's hard to list them all in a few paragraphs. Less fat, more muscle, less depression, more happiness, less grey, more colour, less tiredness, more energy, less ageing, more drive, less loneliness, more sex. Need I say more?

On top of these benefits, if you put on your trainers and get your heart rate up, you'll get more clients. Yes, exercise will get you more clients. A study in the *Journal of Labour Research* found that people who exercise generate 9% more income than those who don't.

Most of us spend too much time sitting at our desks, driving cars and sitting on the train. You need to get up and move. It doesn't matter what exercise you do, as long as you enjoy it and try to do it three to five times a week. If you like cycling, jump on the exercise bike twice a week and go for a long ride at the weekend. If you enjoy weight training, get to the gym every morning or if you can't, put some dumbbells in your office and do some reps at lunch.

If you're travelling, book a hotel with a gym. If the hotel doesn't have a gym, take resistance bands or a suspension trainer and exercise in your room. Or, even simpler, put on your running shoes and go for a jog. There is no excuse; just get it done.

Step 5—Wear Good Clothes

Mark Twain said, "The clothes make the man. Naked people have little or no influence on society." The look and feel of the attire you choose will have a direct correlation with how a client perceives you. If you dress cheaply, you'll attract cheap clients. It's better to have one or two expensive suits than five or six cheap ones. Look at it as an investment: the money you lay out on a proper suit will pay for itself many times over.

Of course, you need to make sure you have good shoes to

match. Nothing too fashionable, but a conservative, well-kept clean pair of shoes. A good suit and shoes make you feel like a millionaire, and that confidence will help you attract more model clients.

Step 6—Eat Nutritious Food

Get nutritious food in you. You are what you eat, so eat the right things in the right quantities as if your life and bank balance depended on it. Both do.

Look at your plate of food and ask yourself, "Will this make me look good in my expensive new suit?" and "Is there colourful, nutritious food in front of me?" If the answer is 'no' then don't put it in your mouth.

I'm not a nutritionist and you should talk to a doctor before changing your diet, but deep down, you already know what is right for you and what isn't. It's common sense. A good place to start is by reducing food that is beige: crisps, chips, bread, pasta and biscuits have lots of calories but not much nutrition.

Some foods are colourful but only through additives, so think twice about sweets, cakes, fizzy drinks and processed cereals. They might taste good and give you a short-lived sugar rush, but as sure as night turns to day your body will crash a few hours later. What goes up must come down.

You know what food is right for you and what isn't. Unless you're an Olympic athlete none of us is going to eat 100% healthily; we live in the real world. A few treats won't do you any harm as long as they're just that: an occasional treat.

Step 7—Go To Sleep

Get plenty of sleep. If you're exercising, dressing well and eating the right foods in the right quantities, none of it will do you any good unless you get enough sleep. My number one personal power is to get up early, which means I also need to go to bed early.

Most scientists agree that adults require between seven and eight hours of sleep. So, if you want to seize the day by getting up at 5 am you'd do well to hit the sack around 9:30 pm. If you're going to get up at a more manageable 6 am then its lights out at 10:30 pm.

You might think eight hours is too much. It is, after all, a third of a day. That's a big lump of time when you're losing opportunities to get things done. Wrong. Just think about what happens when you sleep. Your eyes close, you become unconscious and your mind paralyses the body. You're vulnerable when you're asleep. Thousands of years ago your distant ancestors also slept at night, but they did it at a time when there was a real risk of them being attacked by another human or wild animals. If early humans took the risk of sleeping, we could assume that it must be essential for us to do so. We must sleep, or we don't function. It's not a luxury; it's an absolute necessity.

Scientists haven't figured out why we sleep, but they are starting to conclude findings from recent studies. As you learn new things and encounter new experiences during the day, your brain cells build connections to other parts of the brain. When you sleep, your brain reorganises itself to strengthen the critical bonds and trim back the unimportant.

On top of this reorganising, the brain also 'empties the trash' when sleeping. During the day, waste chemicals build up in the brain and at night these are transported out while we are inactive.

Think of your brain as your office desk. There are post-it notes strewn all over the place. When you sleep, you record and log the important notes and put the remaining ones in the bin. When you don't get enough sleep, the post-it notes build up, and it becomes all too easy for you to lose track of all your ideas, thoughts and reminders. It becomes difficult to concentrate and work on the important stuff.

When you're tired, it's hard to think straight. Subconsciously, you force parts of the brain to shut down even when you are awake. So here's the question: do you want to meet clients with parts of your brain inactive? What kind of impression will that make? Your wellbeing is essential to getting more clients, and your sleep is vital to your wellbeing.

Step 8—Learn From Failure

Whoops! Argh! Oh bother! Oh shoot! Damn! F**k! What do you say when you make a mistake? And why do so many of us try to do everything we can to avoid them? Being yourself means being tolerant of the mistakes you make so you can learn from your failures.

"The fastest way to succeed," IBM's founder Thomas Watson Snr said, "is to double your failure rate." Many industries and thought leaders now recognise that failure can be a good thing—in fact, it's often a precursor to discovery. It will be challenging to find and engage your personal power if you're not willing to take risks and learn from the subsequent mistakes. However, while it's essential to take risks now and then, that doesn't mean throwing caution to the wind or abandoning good practices.

Allowing yourself to make mistakes may seem counter-intuitive. But there's strong evidence that it's good for us. When Jack Welsh was head of General Electric, he said, "We reward failure", explaining that to do otherwise would quash daring.

I once managed to get myself invited to a sales meeting with a prestigious consulting firm. It was the kind of opportunity that could double my revenue; it was a big deal. I was to present my thoughts on how I could help them increase their sales performance and, although I'd run a few big consultancies, this was a different league. What could I add to the party? They already had a team of trainers and on-line courses on sales; surely they had everything they needed?

I was worried that my proposal would be scoffed at or met with an uncomfortable silence. However, I drew on my personal power of not being afraid of failure. I worked hard to be well prepared for the meeting and left nothing to chance. My proposal was good, and I was confident that my solutions would create value for them. I would give it everything I had, and if they decided not to work with me, it was their loss, not mine.

The meeting went as planned, and the client offered me a contract to coach the partners and directors to better sell their services. However, I turned the assignment down. Why? The client's characteristics, behaviour and culture didn't align with mine, and I quickly realised they were not my ideal client. As hard as it was not to take the money, I knew that in the long run the relationships and outcomes wouldn't be as good as they could and should be. I took a risk, prepared, and addressed my fear of failure, but it didn't work out. And that's fine. I learned a lot from my experience and have incorporated the knowledge into my approach. I stood by my principle of working only with model clients and saved myself from a whole lot of pain further down the line.

That is the power of failure—to try new things and learn from the experience, to become better and more resilient.

It is not the critic who counts; not the man who points out how the strong man stumbles, or where the doer of deeds could have done them better.

The credit belongs to the man who is actually in the arena, whose face is marred by dust and sweat and blood; who strives valiantly; who errs, who comes short again and again.

There is no effort without error and shortcoming; but who does actually strive to do the deeds; who knows great enthusiasms, the great devotions; who spends himself in a worthy cause.

Who at best knows, in the end, the triumph of high achievement, and who at the worst, if he fails, at least fails while daring greatly.

So that his place shall never be with those cold and timid souls who neither know victory nor defeat.

FROM "THE MAN IN THE ARENA" BY PRESIDENT THEODORE ROOSEVELT, 1910

Mistakes can teach you how to be truthful to yourself. It's natural to want to cover up mistakes or be embarrassed by them, to feel like pressing 'ctrl-alt-delete' to erase the experience. But being honest about failures can offer an opportunity to hold up a mirror. They teach us, through analysis and feedback, about what works and what doesn't.

I understand that although you can gain a lot from failure, it doesn't feel nice when it happens. However, as much as we might not like the immediate experience, once the dust has settled and you're in the right frame of mind, you might come to appreciate what failure brings. View your failures as gifts, nuggets of gold, a field of diamonds. Embrace your mistakes, your screw-ups, and your f**k-ups, as they provide powerful lessons.

Step 9—Keep On Going

Taking action is powerful; it's the key ingredient to making your revenue grow. Think of a loaf of bread without yeast. It wouldn't rise. Persistence is the 'yeast' for getting more clients and the success of your whole business.

If you leave the vital ingredient of persistence out, very little will come to fruition. Yes, you may start lots of things, but without perseverance you won't achieve many of your tasks and goals. Your power is in the actions you've completed, not the ones you've started. It's not in the number of ideas you come up with—dreamers can think of thousands—and it's not in the volume of tasks you start. Your power comes from focused, determined work to complete the actions that are important to your business success.

Here's an impressive set of numbers to highlight why persistence is so important when it comes to selling your services. Did you know that:

48% of salespeople never follow up with a potential client

25% of salespeople make a second contact then give up

10% of salespeople make three or four contacts

5%, make more than five contacts with a potential client

Why do so many people not continue to make regular contact with their potential clients? They're missing the personal power of persistence. The whole sales cycle for selling consulting and coaching is based on building trust and confidence. Not many of us are capable of establishing high levels of credibility after one or two meetings.

I coach my clients to use the time when their prospects don't need their services to build that critical element of trust. Then, when a client does need your support, you'll have already been in regular contact and established a good relationship. This way, the conversation is focused on how you can help them and add value rather than having to delve into your sales spiel to convince them you're capable of doing the job.

Be persistent. Contact your potential clients once a month, not to sell but to provide useful information and establish relationships. With each contact you'll learn about them, their challenges and ambitions. Every contact brings new learning and moves them towards hiring you.

Portia Nelson wrote a poem that I think tells the story well:

I walk down the street.
There is a deep hole in the sidewalk.
I fall in.
I am lost ... I am helpless.
It isn't my fault.
It takes forever to find a way out.

I walk down the same street.
There is a deep hole in the sidewalk.
I pretend I don't see it.
I fall in again.
I can't believe I am in this same place.
But it isn't my fault.
It still takes a long time to get out.

I walk down the same street.
There is a deep hole in the sidewalk.
I see it is there.
I still fall in
... it's a habit ... but my eyes are open.
I know where I am.
It is my fault.
I get out immediately.

I walk down the same street.
There is a deep hole in the sidewalk.
I walk around it.

I walk down another street.

Sometimes you'll find it hard to keep going. Potential clients will not return your calls or you'll spend weeks writing an article and nobody will show an interest in it. This is when your personal persistence power comes into play. There will be cycles of success when everything aligns and your business thrives, and there will be cycles of failure when things become undone and it feels like nothing is going right. Try to let go and move on from the bad times to make room for the good times. If you hold on to a problem or refuse to move on from a negative experience, it means you're resisting the normal flow of ups and downs of running a business.

Go further than this: try not to think of the up cycles as good and the down periods as bad. Getting more clients is positive, but nothing can grow forever. If it did, it would become stressful and unsustainable. Ending the cycle of growth and flowing to a down period is necessary. One cannot exist without the other.

Sometimes what you think is a good event can turn out to be negative, and what you consider to be lousy might be the best thing that ever happened to you. Dwayne 'The Rock' Johnson was an up-and-coming football player when he was injured and forced to give up the sport. He moved into wrestling and then on to acting. He says of the day he was injured, "It was the best worst day of my life." He thought his injury would bring his world to an end, but it turned out to be a doorway to a new path.

There's an old Taoist parable that demonstrates this point. An old Chinese farmer lost his best stallion and a neighbour came round to express his regrets. The farmer looked at him, smiled, and said, "Who knows what is good and what is bad?"

The next day the stallion returned, bringing with him three wild mares. The neighbour rushed back to celebrate with the farmer, but the farmer said, "Who knows what is good and what is bad?"

The following day, the farmer's son fell from one of the wild mares while trying to break her in and broke his arm and hurt his leg. The neighbour came by to check on the son and give his condolences, but the farmer just smiled and said, "Who knows what is good and what is bad?"

The next day the army came to the farm to conscript the farmer's son for the war. But they found he had a disability due to his injuries and left him with his father. The neighbour thought to himself, "Who knows what is good and what is bad?"

You might be finding sales hard going at this very moment. You might have called fifty people with no response. Don't let it get you down too much or be too despondent. The power of persistence will get you through to better times. These fifty people not responding might be the best thing that could ever happen to you. As the old farmer said, who knows what is good and what is bad?

Step 10—Empty Your Mind

There are three practices I have found helpful, and they might also help you. They are solitude, silence and stillness. The popularisation of mindfulness has brought these practices to our attention, but how many of us have studied and practised them?

The secret to tapping into your unrealised potential is combining solitude, silence and stillness. Once you take deliberate steps to remove yourself from the business of the world and your mind chatting nonsense, you'll create space in your head for the answers to important questions. Your subconscious mind already knows the solution you need; you just need to create the environment to hear what it's telling you. Buddhists call this practice *Zazen*—to meditate with no pre-set purpose other than quieting the mind and watching what comes to you. You must take time out. It's a necessity, not a luxury. When running a business and conducting intricate work, your mind is like a chessboard of thoughts with an infinite number of choices for what your next move will be.

Giving something your full attention can be impossible and stop you from plugging into your personal power and ultimate potential. *Zazen* helps you strip away your extraneous thoughts, opinions, reflections and ingrained paradigms, allowing you to act on what is essential with superhero qualities.

Imagine sitting in front of a wall of televisions, let's say twenty screens, each on a different channel. One is showing a crime series, another a music video, another is showing a political documentary and another presenting the news. Now take these four screens and multiply by five so you have twenty screens demanding your attention.

How could you ever focus on and understand all twenty sources of information? Noise kills personal power and robs you of the ability to solve challenges and get things done. Solitude, silence and stillness can provide an antidote to today's condition that afflicts so many of us: drowning in a flood of information.

Find somewhere quiet, somewhere where you're confident you will not be disturbed. It's best to have silence—I use a set of noise-cancelling headphones to separate me from the outside world. Switch your phone off or put it in aeroplane mode to make sure you're not disturbed. Think about closing the office door and put a sign on the outside telling people not to come in. You need solitude.

Begin by counting breaths in a motionless, upright, seated position. You don't need to sit cross-legged on the floor, just find a comfortable seat, but not so comfy that you might fall asleep. The process of stilling the bodily functions allows you to quieten the random thoughts bouncing around and strengthens concentration.

Zazen is not meditation in the traditional form, nor is it mindfulness in a modern way. It is simply solitude, silence and stillness. It doesn't involve focusing on a topic or problem or visualising a scenario that needs an answer. It aims to free you from the straitjacket of your thoughts, visions, objections and imaginings. If you do this, the right answers to the right choices will come to you. Bringing yourself to a state of emptiness leads to full self-realisation. It will allow you to find the energy, determination and courage—your personal power—to be the best version of yourself.

Why don't you try it? Find somewhere where you won't be interrupted (solitude), close your eyes and count your breaths to quieten your noisy mind (silence), don't focus on a specific event, sit motionless with an open mind and let the answers come to you of their own volition (stillness). Practise it, and over time you'll come to realise what your personal powers are. Once you've identified them, aim to structure your day and week to incorporate them into your routines.

* * *

Ten Steps To Find Personal Power

Step 1–Use empowering words
Step 2–Pursue balanced wellbeing
Step 3–Get up early
Step 4–Get some exercise
Step 5–Wear good clothes
Step 6–Eat nutritious food
Step 7–Go to sleep
Step 8–Learn from failure
Step 9–Keep on going
Step 10–Empty your mind

APPRECIATING ADVENTURES

What

Don't be like a racehorse galloping towards the finishing line with a set of blinkers on. Loosen up a little, take off the blinkers, look around and enjoy the here and now. If you do, you'll relax and so will the people you are selling to.

Why

How many times have you worked with someone who seems to have it all and yet they are not happy or satisfied? I've met plenty of them in my time, especially owners of small consulting companies and partners of large firms. There's not much point in starting or continuing with your adventure unless you take a little time to appreciate everything around you. If you don't, you run the risk of not being satisfied or happy even if you achieve your ambitions. Remember: happy people sell.

How

Take some time out. It could be five minutes or five hours, but do take the time to appreciate your adventure. Do something fun or silly, accept that there are some things you cannot change, so try not to let your worries take over your life. Focus your energy on the things you can control.

✳ ✳ ✳

I have met so many successful service professionals who have 'made it' but are unhappy. Most are on their second or third spouse, have strained relationships with their children and carry a considerable amount of debt. They have achieved their goal and obtained the financial reward, but they've made too many sacrifices along the way. Their goal has been achieved, but their joy has been fleeting and it hasn't brought them the happiness they imagined. What's the point of putting yourself through all that when the whole experience is miserable?

Your work needs to be based on the things you love to do. Go right back to the first chapter in this book. Who are you? What do you do? Who do you serve? And why do you do what you do? Some of your success will come from the referrals because of the reputation you build. But people will only recommend you if you do superb work, and you'll only do this by doing something you love.

It doesn't make sense to spend the next five or ten years of your professional life working on something you don't enjoy. You won't find satisfaction in providing a service to a target market just because you think you'll make a lot of money from them.

People who strive only to be successful rarely are, because achieving success is not an end in itself. It's an after effect, a spin-off from doing something you love well. Passion and enthusiasm are good things. Obsession is not. If you become obsessed with achieving your business goals to the detriment of everything else, you'll find yourself disoriented and choosing a path that ends up taking you in the opposite direction of living life to the full.

Do you want success at any price, or do you want to be successful by filling your days with love, enjoyment and appreciation? That's where real achievement is found: through enriching your and your client's life.

Step 1—Understand Your Why

Before I agree to work with a new client, I always ask them three questions:

What is your goal, your endpoint?

How focused are you on achieving your goal? What are you willing to give up?

How much effort are you going to put in? How many hours are you going to work?

In answer to the first question people usually give a financial value, and for some reason it's usually a revenue goal of around £3m. I have no idea why, but everyone wants to earn £3m. In answer to questions two and three, people usually say their focus and effort will be 110%. How can anyone give 10% more than is physically possible? What they mean is that they are so focused on their targets that they're willing to subordinate everything else in their life. They're also willing to work all hours to do it.

I don't know if people say this to sound impressive or because they think these are the answers I want to hear. So, I ask them: "Why?" "Why do you want that amount of money, and why are you going to work on your business to the detriment of everything else?"

Why?

Before you set off on your adventure, I would urge you to ask yourself some basic questions.

Why do I want to earn this amount of money?

What am I going to use the money for?

How will this make me happy?

Am I willing to prioritise it over everything else: family, friends, leisure time?

Step 2–Walk The Path

You had or have a stable job with a steady income. You might have a family that is settled and used to your monthly salary. Why would you run the risk of embarking on an adventure to a strange new land and place everything at risk?

Perhaps you took that first step out of a sense of frustration or ambition or a combination of the two. Or because you have an uncontrollable longing for adventure. When you set out, you might be apprehensive, and yet with every step you take you'll surprise yourself with how far you have come, how strong you have grown and how much you're filled with enthusiasm. If you're happy, you're walking down the right path towards your goals.

You might feel frightened at the start of your journey, but that feeling will give way to pride and satisfaction as you perform the work you enjoy and are good at. You'll be using your approach, your techniques and methods, doing things your way. And you'll work with the type of clients you used to dream of before.

You'll meet other consultants and coaches on the same road, experiencing the same feelings. As you talk to them, you'll realise you're not alone. They might become travelling companions and share solutions to common problems. The relationships with your companions may develop so that they become partners and colleagues. And together, with combined knowledge and experience, you'll both feel stronger than you ever thought possible.

The path will become smoother and straighter. Your troubles, fears and concerns will fade, and you'll have the capacity to lift your head high and, for the first time, see with clear eyes the true nature of the business you are in.

You'll have committed to follow your chosen path and will not accept any alternative. You'll discover that your personal power bends events and decisions in your favour.

Even if your destination changes several times during the adventure and you take the wrong turn a few times, your personal power will return you to the right course.

You will continue your journey. Instead of complaining and worrying about your challenges, you'll work to help your clients resolve their difficulties. As you grow tired, you'll rest and enjoy looking over all the great work you have done and how many people you have helped.

Rested and recharged, you will set off again on the next instalment of your great adventure.

Step 3–Do Not Worry

There's nothing wrong with a little anxiety; it's a natural emotion. We want good things to start quicker and bad things to stop sooner. However, we cannot control time. If you're passionate about your business and have a strong desire for more clients, life can feel tense at times. Perhaps you're waiting to hear back from a client who would be perfect to work with, desperate to know if they've decided to go ahead with an assignment. It's easy for a friend, colleague or a member of your family to say, "Don't worry, it will be ok." But it's impossible for someone who has invested so much not to worry.

We're all born with the capability to worry and be anxious. It stays with us until we die. It's a human condition, and while a few of us can overcome it, most of us need to learn how to live with it. Anxiety is as natural to us as happiness or sadness. It's an emotion we need to learn how to manage.

You might not like what I am about to say next, but you should hear it. If you can't learn to live with a little anxiety, your life will be difficult and unpleasant. Most service professionals wish they had an extra two hours in the day to get all their work done. But if you're anxious, those hours—every hour—will be a torment. Even worse, you'll do things to try to reduce your anxiety, but your actions will have the opposite effect. They might even make things worse.

Think of someone waiting for a text or a call from the person they went on a date with the previous night. They look at their phone every five minutes to see if there's a message. Every time they look, willing the phone to ring, their anxiety grows. I suffer from phone anxiety when I'm waiting for one of my teenage children to call or text me to let me know where they are and when they're coming home. When I feel like this, with every hour that passes, my anxiety grows.

In work, anxiety comes from many sources. If you're not careful these anxieties can combine and build to create one insurmountable problem, so much so that it blocks everything else out and you're unable to see the positive things around you.

It's all too easy for a consultant or coach trying to build their business to allow anxiety to creep in. It nudges you, over and over, and you start thinking the worst might happen. This can lead to you losing focus on meaningful work, not exercising, eating the wrong stuff and damaging relationships. When you switch the lights off and go to bed, you'll stare up at the ceiling unable to sleep.

If you allow it to build like a snowball rolling down a hill, anxiety can accumulate and morph into an obsession. Once you're obsessed, you'll look for things that don't exist. Your well-meaning enthusiasm will be replaced by a destructive fixation.

Once obsession takes hold, fear can spread to all aspects of your life, and you'll even feel afraid without knowing why.

Many service professionals know something feels wrong but they can't put their finger on it. It's fear.

People might compliment you on how hard you work and the commitment you show, because you drive yourself so hard out of an unrecognised fear. So, you work even harder, to stop the negative thoughts seeping into your mind. You'll work more and more until there's nothing else in your life.

Although anxiety is a natural part of life, don't let it control you. Don't dismiss it as a 'little stress'. I did once, and I ended up crashing out of work for three years, which affected all the people I cared most for. If you feel the need to take on lots of assignments or work long hours with the mistaken assumption that it will make you productive, stop. Stop and tell yourself and others that you need some time out to refresh and recapture your enthusiasm and inspiration to serve your clients well. Don't worry that your friends, colleagues or clients won't come back to you. Remind yourself that excessive caution destroys the soul of your business. If you've served your clients well, they'll always return.

Anxiety will never totally disappear. Stay in contact with your feelings, take time out to refresh and guard against it. If you can maintain a balanced approach, try as it might, anxiety will not take control.

Step 4—Enjoy The Music

When you play a sport, you can approach it in two ways. You can either play to win, or you can play for the sheer enjoyment of it. Winning gives you a quick boost of mood-lifting dopamine, whereas playing just for the sake of it gives you a more steady release.

Playing to win is a bit like jumping in a car and driving as fast as you dare, battling through the traffic jams, jumping from lane to lane, grinding through the roadworks to arrive at your destination. It's a stressful way to travel, and if you did gain any enjoyment from the journey it would be short-lived.

But if you play to play, it's like taking a beautiful Sunday drive through the countryside in your classic car. You've got no particular destination, you're just driving and taking in the scenery all around. You might go fast when you want to and then slow down to take in the sights, taking a pit-stop every now and then for a coffee or a spot of lunch.

Of course, taking the scenic route to nowhere, while giving you some beautiful experiences, might also distract you and make you lose sight of your goal. Neither option will bring you long-term success. You need to find a third way, a way to win whilst also appreciating your journey towards success. It's essential to set goals and challenges that turn your meandering into a quest with a purpose.

Always have a goal in mind. But remember that it costs nothing to stop now and then as you go along to enjoy the view around you. As you advance step by step down your chosen path, you'll be able to see a little further into the distance. Take these opportunities to discover things you hadn't noticed before. Check in with yourself and judge if you're still upholding your work values and ethics. It's also important to find ways to smell the roses, to absorb all the great things going on around you and enjoy the moment. You can have the best of both worlds: a steady stream of happiness and the occasional rush when you achieve a significant milestone.

You might view your business and your endeavours to get more clients as serious work. We all do. But it won't do any harm to take a softer, more playful view. The philosopher Alan Watts describes how we consider music as playful. We 'play' the piano; we don't 'work' it. Unlike driving a car or playing a game where the objective is to reach a goal, in music the goal isn't to reach the end of the composition. If that were the case, the best musicians would be those who played the fastest, and composers would only write finales. People would go to a concert just to hear the final note.

Most education systems around the world have a goal-driven

approach. A child starts by entering a primary school where they are tested and graded. They're then funnelled into high-school and tested and ranked for GCSEs and A levels. Life is revving up, the end point is coming. They're rushing forwards towards more exams and qualifications. Then the pupil goes to university. They graduate, and when they're through with university they go out to join the big wide world. They're no longer a child but a young adult who has spent most of their life chasing the next milestone.

That graduate continues down the same path, maybe selling consulting services. They have a monthly quota to make and they have to achieve it. The next month comes around, and it starts over with bigger targets, promotion and more work. All the time that 'thing' is coming. It's coming. That great 'thing', the success they're working for.

Then, if they're lucky, one day they wake up at about 40 or 50 years old and they proclaim, "My God, I've arrived. I'm successful. I'm there". But they don't feel very different from how they've always felt.

Look at the people who live to retire. They squirrel their savings away to enjoy at a later day. But when they get to the autumn years, at 65 or 70, they have no energy or spark in them. So, they sell their house, move into a housing complex and waste away.

Many of us think of life as a journey. Some believe there's a serious purpose to it and that the overriding goal is to get to that end. That might be to become a millionaire, achieve fame, start a family, or something else. We can become so focused on our legacy that we cheat ourselves the whole way down the line. We can miss the point for 80 years. Or, if we're lucky, really lucky, we come to realise that life is a music thing, and we're supposed to sing and dance while the music is being played.

Have goals, targets, ambitions and dreams—something, anything to create motion. But sing and dance along the way. Think of your journey as a great adventure and savour every moment.

Step 5–Appreciate the seasons

Within the consulting and coaching arena, there are seasons of growth and retraction. It's natural and, try as we might, we can't ignore the ups and downs of the business cycle.

In spring, you build business plans, create new services and products and design new marketing materials. In summer, everything is in full swing. You're busy supporting existing clients and continue to promote your services to attract a growing list of new ones.

In autumn the pace of work slows. You still have a core list of clients, but your services and promotional materials grow tired and jaded. Then in winter, the cold settles in with no growth or new clients in sight. You're dependent on what you've stored away in preparation for this bleak time.

If you refresh your offerings and plant new seeds, winter's grip will loosen, allowing new shoots to flourish and breath life back into the business. Most service professionals would like to make the warm, busy days of summer last forever. But we all know that too much work, too much sun and heat, will dry things up and create cracks. Both you and your business need periods of rest. You must give way to autumn to recover from the summer frenzy.

Within the business world, and in life in general, there are neither winners nor losers. There are only seasons to be enjoyed. The length of each season might be one month or five years; the duration is determined by the quality of work you invest into the business during spring. If you take the time to plant and propagate healthy seeds, you'll have long summers and short winters.

However, if you skimp during the spring using substandard materials and don't put in the effort to create the right conditions for your services to develop and grow, you'll have short summers and long winters. Whatever season your business is in, if you understand there will be hot and cold cycles, you'll be able to accept the difficult times and not be complacent during the long, warm days of summer. All seasons pass. One will succeed another, and the cycle will continue.

Losing a potential or current client will bring moments of darkness, but this too will pass. You'll discover hidden strengths and your self-respect will return to new heights. Take time out during both the good and bad times to work out what you're doing right and wrong. Use the seasons to your advantage: the autumn and winter moments to rest and heal and spring to devise new strategies and equip yourself better for the next cycle. Appreciate quiet times and try not to worry too much about where your next client will come from. Reflect, recuperate, regrow.

Step 6–Ask These Questions

The life coach Tony Robbins asks himself a set of questions every morning and every evening. I've found them useful to remind me to appreciate the adventure I am on, so much so that I have them printed and stuck on the wall next to my desk. Ask yourself these sets of questions every day and night, coming up with two or three answers for each:

Morning questions

What am I happy about in my life right now?

What am I excited about my life right now?

What am I proud about in my life right now?

What am I grateful about in my life right now?

What am I enjoying most in my life right now?

What am I committed to in my life right now?

Who do I love and who loves me?

Evening questions

What have I given today, or in what ways have I been a giver?

What did I learn today, and how can this help me in the future?

How has today added to the quality of my life? How can I use today as an investment in my future?

I try to ask myself these questions daily, but in all honesty, I probably reflect on them weekly. Asking these questions can remind us where we're going and why we're on this adventure. You might find them useful too.

Step 7–Overcome Your Obsessions

For most of us, in business and in our personal lives, our actions are pre-determined by our genes. We're hard-wired to want more: more money, more fun, more stuff, more success, more clients, more of everything. People are unconsciously driven never to be satisfied.

Our genes make us do things that, in the past, helped our ancestors pass their genes from their generation to the next. We're driven to continue the family line, which means that our impulses are to eat, have sex, earn esteem and overcome our competitors.

In Robert Wright's book *Why Buddhism Is True*, he talks through three principles that explain why our genes drive our actions. Achieving goals brings pleasure. That means that all human beings will work hard to attain things that give us pleasure. The pleasure we experience doesn't last forever. After all, if the joy didn't fade, you wouldn't need to pursue it again. Your first meal would be your last as your hunger would never return. The same applies to sex. Being satisfied with the experience of a single act of passion wouldn't allow your genes to be passed down to the next generation.

The brain focuses on the fact that achieving a goal will bring pleasure. However, that pleasure will dissolve afterwards. If you focus on achieving the goal, you'll pursue things like food and sex and social status with enthusiasm. If you focus on the fleeting nature of pleasure, you might start to ask what the point of chasing happiness is if it dissipates after you get it and only leaves you desiring more.

My first car was an Austin MG Metro. It was a fast little car, and I loved whizzing around town in it with the music turned up full blast. I thought I was the coolest teenager in town. However, I soon became dissatisfied and wanted something bigger, so I bought a Ford Escort, and then a Volvo 440. As my wealth continued to grow, so did my cars. I bought a Mercedes C class, then the larger E class and finally the S class. I was driving one of the biggest and most expensive cars you could buy. I didn't need it, but I wanted it, and when I got it, the buzz I got from driving was intoxicating. It made me feel special—but it faded within a month or two.

Our bodies are addicted to certain hormones, and dopamine is one of them. We're junkies. This makes the anticipation of pleasure very strong but the happiness itself short-lived. Dopamine is released when we get or feel something good. However, over time we receive more dopamine in anticipation of achieving the goal and less from the achievement itself. We receive more dopamine by way of anticipating the pleasure that comes from the actual event.

These examples highlight why we give ourselves goals and chase after them. Our genes tell us to do so; we enjoy the chase. When I ask clients, "What is your goal?" their answer boils down to two things: money and social standing. And they're willing to sacrifice a lot—too much—to get them. Money and standing are not bad things, they're both reasonable goals to aim for. However, what are you going to do with them once you've got them? Holidays, more time with your family, more leisure time, more reading, learning new skills? Here's the rub: the goals you're working so hard for in the hope of enjoying them in the future are the very things you're willing to sacrifice now. They're available to you right now, in abundance, if you'll just take the time to enjoy them. Life is for living in the moment, not for working hard to achieve a material object which will give you only fleeting enjoyment.

Step 8–Relinquish Your Control

It is our emotional experience and our actions that determine how much we'll appreciate our adventure, not what happens to us.

Financial success is to be enjoyed and appreciated, but it's our feelings and experiences that we'll remember when we look back. And our emotional experiences depend on how we react to external events; allowing events to play out without affecting our emotional state is key to finding serenity.

Few things are in our control. Most are not. So, don't concern yourself with trying to change the things you can't. There will be times on your journey when you'll be worried or in pain. They can't be avoided. But how you react to them will determine the amount of suffering you have from the experience. To paraphrase the Buddha, "It is the first arrow that will hurt, everything after that is self-inflicted."

The only things that are fully under our control are our thoughts and actions. Everything else is not, including what others think, do and say. When we try to control a situation or another person, it always results in unhappiness.

God, grant me the serenity to accept the things I cannot change, the courage to change the things I can, and the wisdom to know the difference.

PETER BRODIE

THE ALCOHOLICS ANONYMOUS SERENITY PRAYER, ATTRIBUTED TO REINHOLD NIEBUHR

If we let go of the things we can't command, nothing terrible can happen. It's easier said than done, but accepting that the things outside of you can't be controlled will make life a lot more enjoyable.

Think about the alternative. Aggression, resentment, anger, anxiousness, worry and stress. Trying to control what you can't is a form of self-harm. When you look back on this adventure, what do you hope to feel? I know what I hope for, and I've realised that trying to control things other than my own thoughts and actions will not help me in any way.

Most of us aren't born with the enviable ability to take charge of our emotions and disregard the external environment. So, how do we bring about that positive change within ourselves? The Dalai Lama gave an interview in 1998 in which he outlined five steps: learning, conviction, determination, action, then effort. Learning is crucial as it helps to develop conviction and commitment to change. This conviction develops into determination, which in turn transforms into action. Determination coupled with action provides the impetus for us to make a sustained effort to make changes in our life.

If you're not happy, if something is impeding your adventure, you are the only person who can change that situation through changing your emotions and actions. There is nobody else to blame or come to the rescue; it lies within you.

Imagine you're trying to encourage more people to enquire about your services. After reading this book, you become aware that you've not defined your target market and model client well enough. You've *learned* that promoting your services too wide will dilute your marketing.

But learning alone is not enough. You must increase your awareness of the situation until it becomes a firm *conviction* about the need to focus your marketing efforts. This strengthens your *determination* to *act* by identifying your target market, changing your information materials to reflect their needs and wants, and then directing your communications at this set of people.

Determined *action* enables you to make positive change. No matter the goal or activity you're directing your efforts towards, you must exert the *effort.* This builds a willingness and acceptance to establish new habits to sustain that change and go on to make more.

Step 9—Search For Happiness

Now that we're nearing the end of the book, it's time to take a lighter view. There's a beautiful comedy film called *Hector and the Search for Happiness* that stars Rosamund Pike and Simon Pegg, and in the film, Hector is a psychiatrist who has become weary of his monotonous life. He decides to explore the world to research 'happiness'. He takes notes on his travels to China, Africa and America on what makes people happy. This is what he writes:

> *Making comparisons can spoil your happiness.*
> *A lot of people think happiness means being richer or more important.*
> *Many people only see happiness in their future.*
> *Sometimes happiness is not knowing the full story.*
> *Avoiding unhappiness is not the road to happiness.*
> *Ask yourself, does this person bring you (a) up, or (b) down?*
> *Happiness is answering your calling.*
> *Happiness is sweet potato stew.*
> *Fear is an impediment to happiness.*
> *Happiness is feeling completely alive.*
> *Happiness is knowing how to celebrate.*

Listening is loving.

The last point he recorded, and perhaps the most important, is:

We all have an obligation to be happy.

I like to read this list when work isn't going too well. It cheers me up, and I hope it also does for you.

Step 10–Live Your Life

On a bad day, you might think you're not good enough to be a great consultant or coach. These thoughts can lead you to feel that you're not recognised enough and your talents and skills are unappreciated.

Don't give up on your dreams. There's always hope. Trust that if you work the right amount and stay true to your principles, things will change for the better. Spend your workday promoting your services and explaining what you do to your target market. A client, then another, then another *will* come to find out more about what you offer. And if you've put everything we've covered in this book in place, they *will* ask for your help.

It's all too easy to feel you're useless when times are tough, that you're crawling through a difficult phase of your adventure. That feeling can dissolve self-belief and confidence. Left unchecked, a small voice inside your head can grow louder: "Nobody's interested in your services, you're no good, your clients don't need or want you. You are useless."

Is a flower useless? No, its purpose is to be beautiful. Is a bee useless? No, its purpose is to use the flower to pollinate the food that grows in the ground. Is rain useless? No, its purpose is to water the soil so plants and flowers can grow. Are rivers useless? No, their purpose is to carry the rain back to the ocean to begin the cycle again.

Nothing in the world is useless—including you. Be yourself.

That's enough. It's all you can do, and it's all clients want from you. Take advice from this book, not only to get yourself more clients, but to live the life you've always wanted. Appreciate the adventure.

❋ ❋ ❋

Ten Step To Appreciate Adventures

    Step 1—Understand your why
    Step 2—Walk the path
    Step 3—Do not worry
    Step 4—Enjoy the music
    Step 5—Appreciate the seasons
    Step 6—Ask these questions
    Step 7—Overcome your obsessions
    Step 8—Relinquish your control
    Step 9—Search for happiness
    Step 10—Live your life

THE FRAMEWORK

The 10² Be Yourself Sales Framework

1 - Ten Steps To Build Your Brand

1 - Indentify your market
2 - Define your client
3 - Understand their situation
4 - Define your services
5 - Pinpoint the benefit
6 - Articulate the outcomes
7 - Categorise the outcomes
8 - Explain your purpose
9 - Build your brand
10 - Practice having discussions

2 - Ten Steps To Construct Credibility

1 - Get yourself sorted
2 - Establish a presence
3 - Create some materials
4 - Design a logo
5 - Set high standards
6 - Go beyond expectations
7 - Produce recurring materials

8 - Raise your profile
9 - Change your paradigm
10 - Construct the cycle

3 - Ten Steps To Position Your Pricing

1 - Calculate economy outcomes
2 - Monitise effectiveness outcomes
3 - Monitise efficiency outcomes
4 - Monitise emotional outcomes
5 - Monitise environmental outcomes
6 - Calculate client ROI
7 - Invoice after work
8 - Invoice during work
9 - Invoice before work
10 - Consider offering discounts

4 - Ten Steps To Manage Marketing

1 - Focus your marketing
2 - Creat marketing materials
3 - Connect with friends
4 - Meet new people
5 - Network on LinkedIn
6 - Ask for referrals
7 - Write a book
8 - Use powerful webinars
9 - Manage your marketing
10 - Check your readiness

5 - Ten Steps To Commence Conversations

1 - Ditch the pitch
2 - Establish warm rapport
3 - Dance with them
4 - Project steadfast confidence
5 - Listen to them
6 - Uncover their needs
7 - Establish their interest
8 - State your interest
9 - Confirm shared interest
10 - Agree next steps

6 - Ten Steps To Prepare Proposals

1 - Demonstrate you understand
2 - State the objectives
3 - Set the targets
4 - Quantify financial benefits
5 - Describe the methodology
6 - Provide the options
7 - Establish the timescales
8 - Agree on accountabilities
9 - Get the authorisation
10 - Check the document

7 - Ten Steps To Win Work

1 - Believe in yourself
2 - Indentify their style
3 - Visualise the meeting
4 - Plan the conversation
5 - Brace for objections

6 - Be a salesperson
7 - Avoid these things
8 - Empathise don't sympathise
9 - Say the price
10 - Close the deal

8 - Ten Steps To Plan Progress

1 - Define the goal
2 - Set the deadline
3 - Define the milestones
4 - Plan the activities
5 - Identify the dependencies
6 - Manage the risks
7 - Implement management systems
8 - Take decisive action
9 - Check on progress
10 - Deal with problems

9 - Ten Steps To Find Personal Power

1 - Use empowering words
2 - Pursue balanced wellbeing
3 - Get up early
4 - Get some exercise
5 - Wear good clothes
6 - Eat nutritious food
7 - Go to sleep
8 - Learn from failure
9 - Keep on going
10 - Empty your mind

10 - Ten Steps To Appreciate Adventures

1 - Understand your why
2 - Walk the path
3 - Do not worry
4 - Enjoy the music
5 - Appreciate the seasons
6 - Ask these questions
7 - Overcome your obsessions
8 - Relinquish your control
9 - Search for happiness
10 - Live your life

INDEX

advertising 78, 91
anxiety 228–30
articles 51–2, 81
'assumption' close 174
authenticity 86, 104–5, 158–9, 168
Bacon, Francis 200
Be Yourself framework 14–15, 17, 31, 242–6
benefits 26–9, 62–3, 167; additional 27, 28–9, 31–2; financial 129–133; five Es 28, 31–2, 62–5, 131, 167; primary 26, 28–9, 31, 60, 62–3
biographies 43, 45, 47
books 50; writing 93–6
'Boris Johnson' close 170–2
brochures 43, 51–2, 81
Buddhism 221, 235
business cards 45–6, 86
Carnegie, Dale, *How to Win Friends and Influence People* 49, 104
'clique of 10' 92–3
closing (a sale) 144–5, 166–7; templates 168–87
clothes see dress
confidence 109, 145–6, 159
credibility 36–9
credibility builders 36–9; agreed 37; assumed 37, 39; delighted 38, 48–51; reversed 39; unconcerned 38
customer relationship management system (CRM) 98
Dalai Lama 238
deal or no deal close 180–3
Deming, W. Edward 200
desire (client's) 22, 24, 168
discounting 70–5; bundling 71; demand 73; entry 73; payment 75; volume 72
dress 162, 212–13
elevator pitch 14, 33, 105, 110
email addresses 40, 41
emails 82–4
empathy 85, 148, 164–6
'escalation' close 174–7
exercise 211–12
failure 215–17, 219, 220, 240
fear (client's) 22, 24, 111–12
feedback see testimonials
Gantt charts 196–7, 199
goals 189–90, 199–200, 227, 231, 232, 235–7

247

Goggins, David 204
Goleman, Daniel, Social Intelligence 108–9
'group of 80' 83–4, 92–3
handwritten notes 48–9
happiness 225–6, 239–40
Holmes, Chet, The Ultimate Sales Machine 77
Hoshin Kanri 195–6
invoicing 66–8
Johnson, Dwayne 220
Kano model 37
Kano, Noriaki 37
Kipling, Rudyard 202
LinkedIn 14, 33, 40, 42, 55; company page 42; networking 87–90; profile 42
logos 45–6
marketing 18, 54–5, 77–102; materials 81; 'wide-blast' 18, 79, 83–4
meditation 221–2
meetings: confirmation 50–1; sales 103–18, 149–54, 215–16
methodologies 34, 70, 116, 122, 133–4
metrics 128, 129, 197; driver numbers 197, 198; financial results 197, 199; watch indicators 197, 198
milestones 192–3
mindfulness 221–2
model client 20–1, 32, 91, 92, 115–6, 215–16
money discomfort 163–4
Nelson, Portia 218–19
networking: LinkedIn 84–7; physical 87–91
niche 20, 26
outsourcing 193–4
paradigms 54
Parkinson's Law 191–2
persistence 217
personality types 146–9
photographs 40, 52; professional 40–1
physical appearance 162, 207, 212–13
plan-do-check-act method 188, 200–1
'pocket' close 183–5
Port, Michael 58–9
positive thinking 159–60, 205–7, 240
PR 53–4
pricing 61–75, 116, 154–5, 163, 166
proposals 118, 120–42; accountabilities 138–9; authorisation 139–40; checking 141–2; language 123–4; length 121–2; options 136–7; structure 122; terms and conditions 140–1; timescales 137–8
qualifications 46–7
'quaternary' close 178–9
rapport 106–11, 157–8, 163
referrals 91–3
rejection 169
return on investment (ROI) 65–6, 129–30, 154
'right brain story' close 185–7
risk 194–5
Robbins, Tony 199, 234
'roll of 20' 84, 90–1, 92–3
Rumsfeld, Donald 194
sales funnels 55–6
sales cycle 55–7, 57–60

sales meetings 103–18, 149, 215–16; preparation 149–54
sales 13–15, 158–9, 168–9 objections 154–8; pushy 144–5 see also sales meetings; closing
Sandstrom, Gillian 103–4
'sandwich' close 166–7
service overview documents 43
sleep 213–15
standards of service 47–8
'Stephen Fry' close 172–4
subscription model 68
target market 17–19, 32, 79, 92
ten-by-ten matrix 14, 17
testimonials 43, 44–5, 155
time-for-money mindset 67, 130, 138
Tolle, Eckhart, The Power of Now 205
Tracy, Brian 169
'triple question' close 177–8
'trivial' close 180
trust 58, 82, 103, 117, 148, 218
video 52–3
Walsh, Ciaran, Key Management Ratios 62
Watson, Thomas Snr 215
Watts, Alan 231
webinars 59, 96–7
websites 42
Welsh, Jack 215
Wilde, Oscar 106
Wright, Robert, Why Buddhism is True 235
Zazen 221–2
Ziglar, Zig, Secrets of Closing the Sale 159, 166

ABOUT THE AUTHOR

Peter is the guy you call when you want and need more clients.

He has been a management consultant, a freelance consultant, built his consulting company, and led several large consulting firms.

In his final role within the consulting arena, he was the Managing Partner of a large global Consultancy. His primary objective was to grow the business, which kick-started his relentless search to find the most efficient, effective and ethical approach to getting more clients.
He now dedicates his time to coaching others on how to sell their services without selling their soul. His approach allows consultants, coaches and other service professionals to get more clients authentically and genuinely - by being themselves.

He is a Fellow of the Institute of Sales Management; this is the highest level of membership available. The institute considers people at this rank as:

> *"Fellows of the ISM are highly experienced and extremely influential as sales gurus and communicators; considered as thought leaders within the sales industry."*

He is also a regular contributor for the respected Forbes magazine and website, writing articles on how to sell consulting and coaching. Its magazine has over 6 million readers and website over 19 million.

His Be Yourself Sales approach is so successful that he guarantees to get more clients and increase revenue. If he doesn't, he refunds his fees.

His email address is: peter@byscoachinggroup.com
His website address is: www.byscoaching.group

Printed by Amazon Italia Logistica S.r.l.
Torrazza Piemonte (TO), Italy